INSIGHT FOR
INSIGHTS AND ⌐

MW01108192

A Man of Integrity and Forgiveness

JOSEPH

From the Bible-Teaching Ministry of

CHARLES R. SWINDOLL

INSIGHT FOR LIVING

JOSEPH: A MAN OF INTEGRITY & FORGIVENESS
Bible Companion
From the Bible-Teaching Ministry of Charles R. Swindoll

Charles R. Swindoll has devoted his life to the clear, practical teaching and application of God's Word and His grace. A pastor at heart, Chuck has served as senior pastor to congregations in Texas, Massachusetts, and California. He currently pastors Stonebriar Community Church in Frisco, Texas, but Chuck's listening audience extends far beyond a local church body. As a leading program in Christian broadcasting, *Insight for Living* airs in major Christian radio markets around the world, reaching people groups in languages they can understand. Chuck's extensive writing ministry has also served the body of Christ worldwide and his leadership as president and now chancellor of Dallas Theological Seminary has helped prepare and equip a new generation for ministry. Chuck and Cynthia, his partner in life and ministry, have four grown children and ten grandchildren.

Based upon the original outlines, charts, and transcripts of Charles R. Swindoll's sermons, the Bible Companion text was written by Derrick G. Jeter, Th.M., Dallas Theological Seminary.

Copyright © 2007 by Charles R. Swindoll, Inc.

All rights reserved under international copyright conventions. No portion of this Bible Companion may be reproduced, stored in a retrieval system, or transmitted in any form or by any means—electronic, mechanical, photocopy, recording, or any other—except for brief quotations in printed reviews, without the prior written permission of the publisher. Inquiries should be addressed to Insight for Living, Rights and Permissions, Post Office Box 251007, Plano, Texas, 75025-1007. The Rights and Permissions Department can also be reached at www.insight.org/permissions.

Published By:
IFL Publishing House
A Division of Insight for Living
Post Office Box 251007
Plano, Texas 75025-1007

In 1998 the Bible study guide, written in 1990, was revised by Lee Hough, Th.M., Dallas Theological Seminary, and the subtitle was changed to *Joseph: A Man of Integrity & Forgiveness*. Copyright © 1998 by Charles R. Swindoll, Inc.

Bible study guide titled *Joseph: From Pit to Pinnacle* was written in 1990 by Lee Hough. Copyright © 1990 by Charles R. Swindoll, Inc.

Outlines edited and expanded by Ed Neuenschwander with the assistance of Bill Butterworth. Copyright © 1984 by Charles R. Swindoll, Inc.

Outlines published in 1981 by Insight for Living. Copyright © 1980 by Charles R. Swindoll, Inc.

Original sermons, outlines, charts, and transcripts, Copyright © ℗ 1980 by Charles R. Swindoll, Inc.

Editor in Chief: Cynthia Swindoll, President, Insight for Living
Executive Vice President: Wayne Stiles, Th.M., D.Min., Dallas Theological Seminary
Theological Editor: Brie Engeler, M.A., Biblical Studies, Dallas Theological Seminary
Content Editor: Amy L. Snedaker, B.A., English, Rhodes College
Copy Editors: Jim Craft, M.A., English, Mississippi College
　　Melanie Munnell, M.A., Humanities, The University of Texas at Dallas
Project Supervisor, Creative Ministries: Cari Harris, B.A., Journalism, Grand Canyon University
Project Coordinator, Communications: Dusty R. Crosby, B.S., Communications, Dallas Baptist University
Proofreader: Joni Halpin, B.S., Accountancy, Miami University
Production Artists: Sharon D. Chandler, B.A., German, Texas Tech University
　　Nancy Gustine, B.F.A., Advertising Art, University of North Texas
Cover Design: D² Design Works, adapted by Kari Pratt, B.A., Commercial Art,
　　Southwestern Oklahoma State University
Cover Image: Jeff Barson

Unless otherwise identified, Scripture quotations are from the *New American Standard Bible*® (NASB). Copyright © 1960, 1962, 1963, 1968, 1971, 1972, 1973, 1975, 1977, 1995 by The Lockman Foundation, La Habra, California (www.lockman.org). All rights reserved. Used by permission.

Quotations marked (KJV) are from the King James Version of the Bible.

Quotations marked (MSG) are from *The Message*. Copyright © 1993, 1994, 1995, 1996, 2000, 2001, 2002 by Eugene H. Peterson. All rights reserved. Used by permission of NavPress Publishing Group.

Quotations marked (NIV) are taken from the *Holy Bible, New International Version*®. NIV®. Copyright © 1973, 1978, 1984 by International Bible Society. All rights reserved. Used by permission of Zondervan.

Quotations marked (NLT) are taken from the *Holy Bible, New Living Translation*. Copyright © 1996, 2004. All rights reserved. Used by permission of Tyndale House Publishers, Inc., Wheaton, IL 60189 USA.

An effort has been made to locate sources and obtain permission where necessary for the quotations used in this Bible Companion. In the event of any unintentional omission, a modification will gladly be incorporated in future printings.

ISBN: 978-1-57972-755-0
Printed in the United States of America

TABLE OF CONTENTS

A Letter from Chuck

Dear Friends:

"Incarnate the truth!"

This declaration from one of my favorite seminary professors still rings in my ears. I have repeated it on numerous occasions, encouraging young pastors and my congregation to put on the truth, like a suit of clothes, and make it walk and talk. Abstract truth seems so sterile, like something best studied by men and women in white lab coats. But when we see the truth displayed in flesh and blood, it isn't barren or theoretical; it is alive and practical.

A very long time ago truth ruled in Egypt, no longer dressed in a shepherd's multicolored coat, but wearing the royal robes of a prime minister. As we study the life of this remarkable man, Joseph, we'll discover that he was the embodiment of some of the most significant truths in all of Scripture. When faced with a temptation that could have destroyed his character, he resisted and ran. When mistreated, misunderstood, and forgotten, he forgave. When discouraged and lonely, he remained faithful and upbeat. When promoted to prominence, he maintained his humility. From one chapter to the next, you will literally shake your head in amazement.

That's the way it is when mere humanity personifies divine truth. My prayer is that as you use this Bible Companion you will come to incarnate the same truth.

Chuck Swindoll

Charles R. Swindoll

HOW TO USE THIS BIBLE COMPANION

Just when you think that the roller coaster of life is leveling off for a smooth ride, you hear the clack of the chain pulling you upward. At the top there is a moment of exhilaration. Then comes the white-knuckle plummet to the bottom and the jolting twists and turns.

So how do we keep our equilibrium on such a ride? How do we face the thrilling highs, the disappointing lows, and the unknown bends with grace and integrity? Does your life feel like it might fly off the tracks? Then looking deeply into the life of Joseph will help to ground you—especially as life's roller coaster rumbles around another sharp corner.

Whether you choose to complete this study individually or as part of a group, a brief introduction to the overall structure will help you get the most out of each lesson.

LESSON ORGANIZATION

 THE HEART OF THE MATTER highlights the main idea of each lesson for rapid orientation. The lesson itself is then composed of two main teaching sections of insight and application:

 DISCOVERING THE WAY explores the principles of Scripture through observation and interpretation of the Bible passages and drawing out practical principles for life. Parallel passages and additional questions supplement the main Scriptures for a more in-depth study.

 STARTING YOUR JOURNEY focuses on application to help you put into practice the principles of the lesson in ways that fit your personality, gifts, and level of spiritual maturity.

USING THE BIBLE COMPANION

Joseph: A Man of Integrity and Forgiveness Bible Companion is designed with individual study in mind, but it may be adapted for group study. If you choose to use this Bible Companion in a group setting, please keep in mind that many of the lessons ask personal, probing questions, seeking to elicit answers that reveal an individual's true character and that challenge the reader to change. Therefore, the answers to some of the questions in this Bible Companion may be potentially embarrassing if they are shared in a group setting. Care, therefore, should be taken by the group leader to prepare the group for the sensitive nature of these studies, to forgo certain questions if they appear to be too personal, and to remain perceptive to the mood and dynamics of the group if questions and/or answers become uncomfortable.

Whether you use this Bible Companion in groups or individually, we recommend the following method:

Prayer—Begin each lesson with prayer, asking God to teach you through His Word and to open your heart to the self-discovery afforded by the questions and text of the lesson.

Scripture—Have your Bible handy. We recommend the New American Standard Bible or another literal translation, rather than a paraphrase. As you progress through each lesson, you'll be prompted to read relevant sections of Scripture and answer questions related to the topic. You will also want to look up Scripture passages noted in parentheses.

Questions—As you encounter the questions, approach them wisely and creatively. Not every question will be applicable to each person all the time. Use the questions as general guides in your thinking rather than rigid forms to complete. If there are things you just don't understand or that you want to explore further, be sure to jot down your thoughts or questions.

Special Bible Companion Features

Throughout the chapters, you'll find several special features designed to add insight or depth to your study. These features will enhance your study and deepen your knowledge of Scripture, history, and theology.

GETTING TO THE ROOT

While our English versions of the Scriptures are reliable, studying the original languages can often bring to light nuances of the text that are sometimes missed in translation. This feature explores the meaning of the underlying Hebrew or Greek words or phrases in a particular passage, sometimes providing parallel examples to illuminate the meaning of the inspired Biblical text.

DIGGING DEEPER

Various passages in Scripture touch on deeper theological questions or confront modern worldviews and philosophies that conflict with a biblical worldview. This feature will help you gain deeper insight into specific theological issues related to the biblical text.

DOORWAY TO HISTORY

Sometimes the chronological gap that separates us from the original author and readers clouds our understanding of a passage of Scripture. This feature takes you back in time to explore the surrounding history, culture, and customs of the world in which Joseph lived.

Our prayer is that this Insight for Living Bible Companion will not only help you to dig deeper into God's Word but also provide insights and application for *real* life.

A Man of Integrity and Forgiveness

JOSEPH

FAVORED SON, HATED BROTHER

Genesis 37

THE HEART OF THE MATTER

The life of Joseph is nothing short of remarkable. His biography occupies more space in Genesis than those of Adam, Noah, Abraham, or even of his own father, Jacob. His story begins at age 17 and ends at age 110 (Genesis 50:26). During his long life, Joseph responded to broken dreams and impossible circumstances with faith that propelled him from the pit of slavery to the pinnacle of power. In this lesson, we'll meet Joseph on the cusp of the pit and gain insight into the dangers of being the favored son of a passive father.

DISCOVERING THE WAY

The apostle Paul taught that everything recorded in Scripture was included to either instruct us on how to live, offer encouragement, or provide us with warnings and timely reproofs (Romans 15:4; 1 Corinthians 10:11; 2 Timothy 3:16–17). The lives of the men and women in the Old Testament were relevant for those to whom Paul was writing, and they are just as relevant for us today. As we go through Joseph's story, as recorded in the book of Genesis, we'll discover timely truth for our lives.

But before we meet Joseph, let's take note of three distinct periods in his life.

Birth to age 17 (Genesis 30:24–37:2). If Joseph's life were a storm, this period would be the clouds swelling up to eclipse the sun. His family was in transition—unsettled, moving. The low rumblings of pain and discontent grew in intensity as his family members clashed in jealousy and hatred.

Age 17 to age 30 (37:2 – 41:46). As Joseph entered into young adulthood, the storm finally burst into torrents of rejection and vengeance, threatening to drown him in the rising waters of enslavement and imprisonment.

Age 30 to death (41:46 – 50:26). The last eighty years of his life were sunny. He was blessed with years of prosperity under God's hand. Though Joseph had an opportunity to blot out the sun from his brothers' lives, he blessed them instead.

A BACKDROP OF FAMILY STRIFE

Joseph's home was anything but a place of shelter. In fact, it was a storm center of activity. To make sense of the hurricane that swept over Joseph's life, we must first understand where it began—with his father, Jacob. Except for a few brief interludes of piety, Jacob simply couldn't be trusted. Unfortunately, his lack of integrity and his passivity had dire consequences for his children.

Jacob had two wives, Leah and Rachel, who also happened to be sisters. But he loved Rachel more, which set up a rivalry that resulted in a childbearing competition (Genesis 29:30). Leah was the first to have children. She eventually bore seven: six boys and a girl named Dinah. Rachel, however, was considered barren—a shameful stigma for a woman in those days. So, Rachel gave her servant Bilhah to Jacob to have children through her. Bilhah bore Jacob two sons. Not to be outdone, Leah retaliated by having her servant Zilpah lie with Jacob, and Zilpah bore him two sons (29 – 30). Finally, Rachel herself conceived and bore a son she named Joseph, which means "may He add," expressing her hope that God would give her another son (30:24).

If you do the math, you get one husband, two wives, two concubines, four mothers, eleven sons, and one daughter—all adding up to jealousy, strife, anger, lust, deceit, competition, and secrecy.

Skim Genesis 29:30–30:8. What was the result of favoritism on the relationship between the two sisters, Rachel and Leah? What did Jacob do to try to keep the peace in his household?

_____

_____

_____

What is lacking in a relationship characterized by jealousy?

_____

_____

_____

The Journey to Canaan

By the time Joseph was born, Jacob was no longer a young man. He had worked in Haran for his father-in-law, Laban, but after twenty years of toil and deception by both father-in-law and son-in-law, Jacob decided to move his family back to Canaan, his homeland (Genesis 30:25).

What should have been a time of adventure and joy turned into a series of tragedies. The family's journey to Canaan came to an abrupt interruption in the land of the Hivites at the city of Shechem. There an authority figure in the land raped Jacob's daughter, Dinah (34:1–2).

Incredibly, when Jacob heard about the rape, he didn't do anything! But Dinah's brothers did. They killed the man who raped her, along with every male in the city (34:3–26). Then they looted the town (34:27–29). Jacob responded with some concern . . . but not about the welfare of his daughter. He was worried about his public relations with the surrounding peoples (34:30–31).

Leaving Shechem behind, an opportunity to rejoice appeared on the horizon—Rachel was pregnant again. As they headed south, her second son was born. But another tragedy struck. Shortly after giving birth to Benjamin, Rachel died (35:16–19).

Walking away from the funeral, still grieving over the death of his beloved, Jacob and the family encountered a third tragic situation. Reuben, the oldest son, committed incest with Bilhah, Jacob's concubine (35:22). Jacob knew about it, but again he didn't do anything. No discipline, no correction, no punishment.

Later, on his deathbed, Jacob removed the rights of the firstborn son from Reuben (49:1–4). But where was Jacob when the sin was committed? Why didn't he do something then?

Think back to a time when you should have acted to right a wrong but did not. What happened? Why didn't you get involved?

_____

_____

_____

Describe the consequences of your inactivity. How did you feel about it afterward?

_____

_____

_____

If you could go back and deal with the situation again, what would you do differently?

_____

_____

_____

What started out as an exciting trip home to Canaan ended up as a gauntlet of grief. The final blow came after Jacob reached Hebron, when his father, Isaac, died (35:27–29).

A FAVORED SON

The arrival of Jacob and his family in Hebron brings us to Genesis 37 and the gathering storm in Joseph's life.

 Read Genesis 37:1–11.

Doting on Joseph may have brightened Jacob's world, but it only brought storms to Joseph's. His brothers knew their father played favorites. Of course Joseph's habit of tattling on them did nothing to dispel the billowing clouds.

And then there was the matter of that colorful coat.

Joseph's multicolored tunic was more than just a gift from a loving father. It was a long-sleeved garment worn by the nobility of the day, a symbol of authority and favored status in the family and an excuse from the hard work of shepherding.[1] The other boys were jealous of all that the coat represented. They hated Joseph.

Making matters worse, Joseph boasted of a dream in which he ruled over his brothers (Genesis 37:5–8). Later, he told his family, Jacob included, that all of them would bow down to him (37:9–11).

A PLAN TO KILL JOSEPH

Though he expressed some concern, Jacob still didn't do anything to dispel the darkening clouds of hatred and jealousy surrounding Joseph, ignoring the thundering signs of the oncoming storm.

 Read Genesis 37:12–25.

Jacob closed his eyes to the danger of sending Joseph, alone, to check up on his brothers, who were tending the sheep. Seeing Joseph in the distance, wearing his brightly colored robe, the brothers decided the time had come to pour out their vengeance on the dreamer (Genesis 37:18–19).

Their first plan was to kill him, throw his body into a pit, and cover up the murder with a lie (37:20). But Reuben persuaded them not to kill him, only to put him in the pit. Secretly, he intended to come back and rescue Joseph (37:21–22).

When Joseph reached his brothers they seized him, stripped off his robe, and threw him into an empty water cistern. Then they coolly sat down and ate lunch (37:23–25).

Read Genesis 37:32–33. Why do you think the brothers used the phrase "your son" instead of "our brother"? What might this indicate about the motive behind their actions?

_____

_____

_____

Think about Joseph's family and his own behavior. What reasons did the brothers have for hating him?

_____

_____

_____

What (or who) was at the root of their hatred? (Genesis 37:3–4)

_____

_____

_____

A Caravan to Egypt

Sometime between the capture of Joseph and the meal, Reuben left. He didn't have an opportunity to intervene when Judah had the bright idea of enriching himself from Joseph's hide.

Read Genesis 37:25–36.

While the brothers were eating their meal they happened to look up and see a passing caravan of Ishmaelite traders. Almost as an afterthought, Judah convinced the brothers to sell Joseph for twenty pieces of silver (Genesis 37:25–28).

When Reuben returned, Joseph was gone. To deceive their father, the brothers ripped up Joseph's coat and dipped it into goat's blood. Believing his son had been killed by a wild animal, Jacob mourned deeply (37:29–35).

While Jacob was grieving, Joseph was taken to Egypt and sold as a slave to Potiphar, the captain of Pharaoh's guard (37:36).

When Jacob believed Joseph to be dead, what regrets do you think might have filled his mind? Write a short summary of the ways that Jacob's parenting led directly or indirectly to the actions of his sons.

_____

_____

_____

_____

_____

_____

 STARTING YOUR JOURNEY
Imagine being in Joseph's sandals. You're only 17 years old, and your siblings throw you into a pit, sit down for lunch, and then sell you as a slave. What thoughts would race through your mind? How would you feel?

We may never experience such hatred or endure such savage treatment as Joseph did, but we can learn four important lessons from his experience.

First, *no family is exempt from adversity*. Every family is unique. We come in different shapes and sizes. Yet we all have one thing in common—we all have to deal with adversity and family conflict. We struggle to get along with each other.

How did your family address sibling rivalry and family conflict when you were growing up? List both the positive and the negative aspects, if possible.

_____

_____

_____

_____

_____

Consider your family today. Do you deal with conflict in the same way? What patterns, if any, might you need to change?

_____

_____

_____

_____

Second, *no enemy is more subtle than passivity*. Most passive parents avoid conflicts until one day they explode in anger. Then in a mindless moment they come down hard, propelling children toward anger, jealousy, and hatred. Or, like Jacob, they avoid discipline at all costs. The consequences are equally dire.

How would you characterize your style of parental discipline?

Active				Passive
1	2	3	4	5

Consistent				Inconsistent
1	2	3	4	5

Firm				Wishy-washy
1	2	3	4	5

Calm				Angry
1	2	3	4	5

If you're not happy with the quality of your discipline, make a list of areas in which you'd like to improve.

1. _____

2. _____

3. _____

Third, *no response is more cruel than jealousy.* Solomon was right; jealousy is as "cruel as the grave" (Song of Solomon 8:6 KJV). If we let the seed of jealousy take root within the relationships of our children, it will uproot family harmony and unity. As parents, we must learn to recognize and weed out negative attitudes as well as actions. And we must never forget to water our children with praise when they display positive attitudes.

Some children are compliant like Joseph, while others are head-strong like Reuben. How would you describe the relationships between your children? What can you do to help them improve their relationships with each other?

_____

_____

_____

As parents, we are often tempted to favor the compliant child because he or she is easier to manage. Think about your relationships with your own children. Do you tend to favor one child over the others? If so, how has that affected your relationships with your other children?

_____

_____

_____

Fourth, *no condition is more unfair than slavery.* Joseph didn't deserve to be enslaved, but he was. Cut off from his father, forgotten by his brothers, it seemed as if Joseph would be lost forever. But God knew exactly where Joseph was, and He was already preparing to raise Joseph from the pit to the pinnacle.

Regardless of our family backgrounds or how we were reared, Joseph's story offers us practical exhortations. His relationship with his father and brothers serves as a siren, warning us against passivity and favoritism and the storms of jealousy and anger that result. In response to this lesson, look to the skies of your family relationships and work to dispel the dark clouds of discontent with the sunlight of firm and loving discipline.

GENERAL OVERVIEW OF JOSEPH'S LIFE

From Pit to Pinnacle
Genesis 37–50

Rejected and Humbled "The Pit"

Promoted and Exalted "The Pinnacle"

	GENESIS 37	to	40	GENESIS 41	to	50
Role	Son . . . Shepherd . . . Slave . . . Prisoner			Governor/Prime Minister of Egypt		
Experience	Envied and Hated / Tempted and Misunderstood / Imprisoned and Forgotten			Remembered . . . Promoted . . . Honored		
Time	Birth to 17: With his family (Genesis 37:2) / Age 17: Sold as a slave / Ages 17–30: Slave and prisoner in Egypt for over 2 years			Began: Age 30 (Genesis 41:46)		Died: Age 110 (Genesis 50:26)
Family	Son of Jacob and Rachel					
Illustration of Christ	Humbled . . . but later exalted (Philippians 2:5–11)					
Application for Christians	Humble yourself so God may exalt you (1 Peter 5:6–10)					

Copyright © 1980, 2006 by Charles R. Swindoll, Inc. All rights reserved worldwide.

11

Resisting Temptation

Genesis 39:1–20

THE HEART OF THE MATTER

Expressing the cynical sentiments of many, Oscar Wilde wrote, "The only way to get rid of a temptation is to yield to it. Resist it, and your soul grows sick with longing for the things it has forbidden to itself."[1] Doubtless, yielding to temptation is much easier than resisting it. But for those who yield, the path of life is strewn with the litter of remorse and shame. Their souls grow sick, not from longing to taste forbidden fruit but for having tasted it. If we wish to avoid such soul sickness, we must resist temptation. But how? Joseph provides a sterling example of one who could have cuddled lust and enjoyed its warm embrace but instead chose to resist its persistent, alluring offer in favor of righteousness.

DISCOVERING THE WAY

Dietrich Bonhoeffer warned that "In our members there is a slumbering inclination towards desire which is both sudden and fierce," and if we give in to these desires, "the powers of clear discrimination and of decision are taken from us."[2]

Every person who has cast a shadow across the earth, including Jesus, has faced temptation. And every person who has ever lived, except Christ, has yielded to it.

Temptation's appeal to our desires is lust disguised with many different masks.

13

Material temptation is the lust for things. *Personal temptation* is the lust for status. *Sensual temptation* is the lust for physical pleasure. In this lesson, we will focus on sensual temptation—the temptation to enjoy another's body when such pleasure is not legally or morally permissible.

We live in a sex-saturated society. There's no escaping that fact. So learning to resist sexual temptation, as Joseph did in Genesis 39, may save our reputations and even our lives.

THE HISTORICAL SITUATION

Joseph's journey to slavery in Egypt eventually led him to a place of prominence . . . and of danger.

 Read Genesis 39:1–6.

Joseph didn't have to tell his master that the Lord was with him, causing his success. Potiphar could see that for himself. Nor did Joseph seek favors from Potiphar. The Egyptian was a shrewd man who recognized Joseph to be diligent and trustworthy, so he promoted Joseph to manage all of his business and household affairs (Genesis 39:5–6).

But behind Joseph's success—his increased responsibility, trust, and freedom—lurked great danger.

In your own experience, when does temptation usually come— when life is good or when it's difficult? Why do you think this is the case? Describe one example below.

_____

_____

_____

Read Matthew 26:41 and 1 Peter 5:8–9. When should we be on guard against temptation?

_____

_____

_____

This brief narrative of Joseph's professional life in Genesis 39:1–6 closes with a personal but crucial aside: "Now Joseph was handsome in form and appearance" (39:6).

THE SENSUAL TEMPTATION

While Potiphar set his sights on Joseph's business acumen, Mrs. Potiphar had her eye on Joseph's well-built body and good looks.

 Read Genesis 39:7–12.

"Lie with me" (Genesis 39:7)—now that's a direct approach! Joseph's refusal was as straightforward and abrupt as the appeal of Potiphar's wife (39:8). He must have been acutely aware of the consequences of succumbing to sexual temptation: he stated them clearly in his response. He refused to have sexual relations with her because it would violate the trust he had with his master (39:8). But more importantly, it would violate his conscience and defame the character of his God (39:9).

Similarly, one way we can avoid falling into sexual sin is to review the consequences of our actions beforehand. In the chart below, briefly but specifically describe the potential effects of sexual compromise relative to each element on the left.

The Lord	
Your spouse (or future marriage relationship)	
Your children	
Your reputation	
Your health	
The other person	
Other areas not listed	

But Mrs. Potiphar wasn't persuaded by Joseph's reasoning. She wasn't interested in the sanctity of her marriage. She wasn't interested in the loyalty between master and slave. She wasn't interested in what God thought. She was only interested in gratifying her desires with Joseph.

Joseph faced a difficult dilemma. The place where he lived and worked brought him face-to-face with seduction. This woman's advances must have been flattering, and they surely aroused powerful sexual desires in Joseph. After all, "Joseph was not a stone, a mummy, but a red-blooded young man in his late twenties."[3] Her allure might have been easy to dismiss if it happened only once, but it didn't—she pursued him day after day (Genesis 39:10) and always when they were alone (39:11).

With each advance, Joseph refused. But one day Mrs. Potiphar resorted to more than just words . . . she grabbed him (39:12). So Joseph ran.

What do 1 Corinthians 6:18–20 and 2 Timothy 2:22 tell us about how we should react to sexual temptation?

_____

_____

_____

According to 2 Timothy 2:22, what should we run after instead?

_____

When we're faced with sensual temptation, we can't reason with it. We can't even stand there and quote Bible verses. All we can do is run — flee — escape. If we stay, we're likely to give in.

 DIGGING DEEPER
The Danger of Internet Pornography
There is no greater danger to an idle mind than the Internet. Though it has potential to enrich our thinking, it has the power to corrupt it as well. Each month thousands of new pornographic sites are created. Don't be fooled into thinking that just one look won't hurt or that your behavior is harmless. Like a spider's web, the images stick in the mind, trapping victims until their life is sucked out by the spider of addiction.

And let's not make the mistake of assuming that the web of pornography allures only men. Women are often attracted to the flickering light of virtual sex too. And given the right set of emotional conditions, exchanges with an anonymous man via e-mail can evolve into much more. An emotional affair, fed by false intimacy, incubated in the secrecy and anonymity of cyberspace, can stifle a pure mind just as quickly as lurid images.

Continued on next page

17

Continued from previous page

If you or someone you love is caught in the web of sexual sin, don't be deceived into believing that these habits will just go away. Address them directly. A variety of excellent books, support groups, and counseling programs exist to help people recover from the devastation and shame of sexual sin. Additionally, Insight for Living provides the services of staff pastors and a women's counselor. Written correspondence or phone consultation is available at no charge. For contact information, please see page 139.

The Personal Ramifications

We might assume that once Joseph made it outdoors, overcoming temptation, he would have heard angels singing his praises and would have been at peace. Instead he heard screams from a rejected and lust-filled woman who wanted nothing but revenge—hurling him from the heights as Potiphar's overseer to the depths as Potiphar's prisoner.

 Read Genesis 39:13–23.

The other slaves came running when they heard Mrs. Potiphar scream. Quickly, she conjured up a lie that Joseph tried to rape her, and she had the "evidence" to prove it. He left his coat. He ran away (Genesis 39:13–15).

When Potiphar came home, she repeated the story. On the surface, it appeared that Potiphar believed her—"his anger burned" (39:19). But perhaps he didn't believe her completely. As captain of the bodyguard, Potiphar may have been the chief executioner and the one responsible for punishing crime throughout Egypt.[4] As Joseph's master, he could have done as he pleased; killing a slave who attempted to rape his wife wouldn't raise any Egyptian's eyebrows. But Potiphar didn't kill Joseph; he placed him in prison. And not just any prison. Joseph was put into Potiphar's prison, the place "where the king's prisoners were confined" (39:20).

Imagine how Joseph must have felt! He had never read the book of Genesis—he didn't know how all of this would turn out. All he knew was that he had done the right thing and he ended up in jail. But God was with him and prospered him. Just as he ruled over Potiphar's house, so he ruled over the prison (39:21–23).

STARTING YOUR JOURNEY
Joseph's life provides us with four important insights to help us say no when our lust says yes.

Don't be weakened by your situation. Joseph was in a position that could have easily undercut his resolve to say no to lust. He was handsome and alone. He enjoyed a secure and trusted position. His accomplishments made him the object of much praise. And, most dangerously, he had complete autonomy.

Under what circumstances are you most vulnerable to sexual temptations (for example, when you're lonely, depressed, sick, tired, or even when you're successful or happy)? Be specific.

_____

_____

_____

One of the best ways to avoid being in a weakened situation is to live our lives in honest, open relationships with other people. When we share our struggles with other trusted believers, we expose the shame of sin, and its pull on us is weakened. Fellow believers can help point out blind spots and can hold us accountable to do the right thing.

Do you make yourself accountable to people who can spot a lie and will call you out on it? If so, to whom? How often do you meet with this person/group?

_____

_____

_____

How thoroughly do you allow your life to be examined? The following questions might be useful as you and your partner(s) hold each other accountable, ideally on a weekly basis.

- Have you been with a woman or man anywhere that might be seen as compromising?

- Have you exposed yourself to any sexually explicit material?

- Have you had a conversation or correspondence with anyone that would make your spouse feel threatened?

- Have you spent adequate time in study of the Scriptures and in prayer?

- Have you given priority to your family?

- Have you just lied in your answer to any of the above questions?

Also, don't forget to celebrate your successes! You'll be encouraged as you see God working in each others' lives.

Don't be deceived by persuasion. Mrs. Potiphar was bold and calculating, and her proposition was tantalizing. No doubt her verbal enticements were as loosely clad and suggestive as she probably was. Each day she tried to lure Joseph with just the right combination of tempting words—"My husband doesn't meet my needs." "Who will find out?" The longer we stand around looking and reasoning, the harder it is to run or even walk away.

What types of persuasion (words, sounds, sights, or touch) are most likely to tempt you into moral compromise?

_____

_____

_____

Sensual temptations surround us, whether they are faceless images or people we interact with daily. What can we do to "flee" from these situations? In the chart below, suggest some barriers or plans of escape for each tempting situation on the left.

Advertising	
Entertainment	
An attractive coworker or friend	
Internet pornography, e-mail, pop-ups, or chat rooms	
Fantasy relationships	
Any other area of weakness you've identified	

Don't be gentle with your emotions. Our emotions will beg and plead for us to open the door to the thrill of temptation. But we must learn to keep it closed tightly! Remember, Joseph refused and called her temptation a "great evil" and a "sin against God" (Genesis 39:9). Then he ran!

Read each of the following Scriptures. What insights can you draw from each passage that might help you control your emotions when faced with sexual temptation?

1 Corinthians 9:24–27

_____

_____

_____

2 Corinthians 10:5

_____

_____

_____

1 Timothy 4:7–8

_____

_____

_____

Don't be confused by the immediate results. Joseph was thrown into prison for doing what was right. For all he knew he would spend the rest of his life rotting there. Yet, as hard as it is to believe, it was in God's plan for Joseph's life. And through that experience, he eventually became ruler over all Egypt.

We owe it to our character, to our families, and to the reputation of Jesus Christ to resist sexual temptation — no matter the cost.

Matthew 5:29–30; 18:8–9; and Hebrews 12:3–4 emphasize the seriousness of sin. Is your goal to not sin very much or to not sin at all? How far are you willing to go to remain sexually pure?

_____

_____

_____

Read 1 Corinthians 10:13. Should we fear temptation? Why, or why not?

_____

_____

_____

The late Swedish diplomat and former secretary-general of the United Nations Dag Hammarskjöld astutely observed, "He who wants to keep his garden tidy doesn't reserve a plot for weeds."[5] The battle to stay sexually pure is hard-fought, particularly in our culture. But the example of Joseph teaches us that resisting sensual temptation is possible—with God's help, we *can* overcome!

LESSON THREE

IMPRISONED AND FORGOTTEN
Genesis 39:20 – 40:23

THE HEART OF THE MATTER
Aleksandr Solzhenitsyn and Elie Wiesel are two men who understand the depth of unjust suffering. They give voice to those who were imprisoned and forgotten in Soviet gulags and Nazi concentration camps. For some, like Solzhenitsyn, these man-made hells helped bring about spiritual conversion. For others, like Wiesel, the hellish experience reduced faith to a heap of ashes.

Joseph knew intimately the depths of hurt caused by injustice. But, although he was sold as a slave, slandered, thrown in prison, and forgotten, he didn't come to the same conclusion as Wiesel. Instead, he chose to unwaveringly trust in God, no matter the injustice. And his example is an inspiration for us. When we face the dark days of discouragement, we too can place our trust and hope in the living Lord.

DISCOVERING THE WAY
The pain of unjust suffering is one of the most severe trials we can experience. And in our world today, it's simply inescapable.

As difficult as injustice is to endure, the greater challenge is facing it with an attitude that preserves faith. Viktor Frankl, another survivor of the Holocaust, saw in his suffering a freedom, which gave him hope. "Everything can be taken from a man," he wrote, "but one thing: the last of the human freedoms—to choose one's attitude in any given set of circumstances, to choose one's own way." [1]

For the most part, what will happen to us today or tomorrow, whether fair or foul, is beyond our control. But we *can* choose our attitude.

Read 1 Peter 2:20. What attitude does God want us to have when we are in the midst of suffering? What is God's response to such an attitude?

MISTREATMENT: COMMON TO EVERYONE

Joseph is a perfect example of someone who did what was right and suffered unjustly. From freedom to slavery to imprisonment, Joseph progressively lost his liberty. Everything about his situation pointed to the conclusion that he was forgotten by God and everyone else. Joseph was left with only one freedom—the freedom to choose his attitude.

During his life, Joseph experienced types of mistreatment that are common to everyone. Perhaps you will recognize them in your own life or in the lives of your family or friends.

Undeserved treatment from family. Even the healthiest families experience the pain of mistreatment among their members, because parents and children aren't perfect. We've all been hurt by the actions of a brother, sister, or parent. And the pain is especially great because of the love we expected to receive from them. Joseph certainly knew this pain; he was thrown into a pit and then sold into slavery by his brothers.

Unexpected restrictions from circumstances. Life is not always fair. Sometimes we are limited by people or situations that are beyond our control. The inability to improve our circumstances or seek justice is irksome and often frustrating. Joseph knew well the weight of the manacles of slavery and imprisonment.

Untrue accusations from people. None of us live very long before we suffer the mistreatment of a wagging tongue. James aptly described the tongue as a fire (James 3:5–6). It only takes a careless spark of untruth to ignite an inferno that can incinerate a reputation. Mrs. Potiphar's lying tongue resulted in Joseph being falsely accused of rape and thrown into prison.

Of these three types of mistreatment, which one is the most real to you and the most painful? Why?

_____

_____

_____

Briefly describe a time when you were mistreated in one of these three ways. What happened? How did you respond?

_____

_____

_____

Imprisonment: Joseph in Jail

The Bible is not a book of fantasy or fiction. It chronicles the lives of real people in real-life situations. Only two chapters into this study, Joseph had already endured abuse from his brothers, the injustice of slavery, and the loss of his reputation. Now he had fallen to the very bottom of the pit — the dungeons of Egypt.

 Read Genesis 39:20–23.

We breezily talk of God's grace and blessing when things are easy, but what about when things are hard? Where was God through all the injustice in Joseph's life? Genesis 39:21 tells us that "the Lord was with Joseph." He was right there in the prison with him.

And we never hear of Joseph doubting God's presence. He chose to wait patiently on the Lord, and God provided him with inner peace as well as favor in the eyes of the chief jailer (Genesis 39:22–23).

Read Isaiah 40:27–31 and summarize it in your own words.

_____

_____

_____

_____

What does this passage promise to those who suffer injustice but wait upon the Lord?

_____

_____

_____

A false accusation landed Joseph in prison, and though he had to live with the physical restrictions, he didn't have to live under emotional or spiritual confinement. Joseph chose to trust in God. He accepted his circumstances. If the Lord wanted him in prison, that was His sovereign right—Joseph accepted God's plan without anger, argument, or agitation.

TWO DREAMS, ONE HOPE

Because of his attitude of trust, God used Joseph strategically in the lives of two important men.

 Read Genesis 40:1–8.

One day, while Joseph was going about his work in the prison, the doors suddenly flew open and two new prisoners were thrown in—a cupbearer and a baker. We're not told exactly what these men did to offend Pharaoh, but chances are it had something to do with the royal food service. The baker prepared meals, while the cupbearer was Pharaoh's taster, preventing poisoned food and wine from being placed before the king. He occupied an especially trusted role in Pharaoh's service.

One night, both men had vivid dreams. Joseph assured the cupbearer and baker that the interpretation of dreams belonged to God, and Joseph offered to help them (Genesis 40:5–8).

Often when our attitudes are positive and we're trusting God, even if we are in the pit of our circumstances, we are more sensitive to others' needs. Describe a time when you were able to help someone in need in spite of your own struggles . . . or a time someone who was suffering helped you.

_____

_____

_____

Read 2 Corinthians 1:3–5. How is this more evidence that God is present with us as we go through suffering?

_____

_____

_____

Notice that Joseph's concern for the baker and cupbearer nudged the dominoes that toppled toward his release.

 Read Genesis 40:9–19.

Joseph encouraged the men to share their dreams. The cupbearer told Joseph about squeezing grapes into a cup and placing the cup in Pharaoh's hand. Joseph interpreted the dream and told him in three days Pharaoh would pardon him and restore him to his position (Genesis 40:9–13).

Joseph may have had a positive attitude, believing God would eventually rescue him from the dungeon, but he didn't live in a dream world. When he asked the cupbearer to put in a good word for him with the king (40:14), he had reason to expect that the cupbearer would remember and help him.

And, as difficult as it must have been to tell the baker of his doom, Joseph had too much integrity to give false hope.

 Read Genesis 40:20–22.

Three days later, just as Joseph had predicted, the cupbearer was restored and the baker was put to death. Now that the cupbearer was returned to his place of trusted service, surely he wouldn't forget what Joseph had done for him.

ABANDONMENT: JOSEPH FORGOTTEN

Joseph had always trusted in God, but now he also trusted in a man. And like others who have hung their hopes on people, Joseph was abandoned—cast into the abyss of the forgotten.

 Read Genesis 40:23–41:1.

We tend to rush past the first part of Genesis 41:1 to get to Pharaoh's dream, but instead let's focus on the beginning of the verse. Joseph, after asking the cupbearer to mention to Pharaoh the miscarriage of justice in his case, sat waiting in prison for two full years.

Two important observations can be made here. First, *Joseph was abandoned by a friend.* If an enemy abandons you, who cares? What else would you expect? But when a friend forgets you, it cuts deeply. Second, *the abandonment was for a lengthy period of time.* If Joseph only had to wait a few days, or a few weeks, it would have been no big deal. But two full years? From his perspective, it probably felt like a lifetime.

Earlier, we addressed three different types of mistreatment. And we can now add a fourth: *Unfair abandonment by one you helped.* Perhaps you've been left by a mate, deceived by a friend, or let down by an employer. Our natural response to this kind of mistreatment is to feel disillusioned, betrayed—first by the person who abandoned us, then by God.

Read the following verses, and note how Jesus was betrayed or abandoned by His friends during the last days of His ministry.

Matthew 26:38–40

Matthew 26:55–56

John 18:4–5

John 18:25–27

Now, read Luke 23:33–34 and 1 Peter 2:21–24. How did Jesus respond to being mistreated? What did He choose to do, even for the people who let Him down?

If you are interested in knowing more about how God is present during our suffering and about the significance of the sacrifice that Jesus made for all people—including you—please read "How to Begin a Relationship with God" at the end of this Bible Companion.

If a struggling friend were to ask you what it means to entrust oneself to "Him who judges righteously" (1 Peter 2:23), what would you say? What must someone believe about God and suffering in order to do this?

———————————————————————————————————

———————————————————————————————————

———————————————————————————————————

STARTING YOUR JOURNEY

The pain and frustration of disillusionment and mistreatment need not lead to cynicism, especially if we understand the cause of our disappointment and learn to embrace and apply the cure.

First, *the cause of disillusionment is putting our complete hope and trust in people.* Like Joseph, we hope people will remember and help us out of the pits in which we find ourselves. Yet, when we put fallible people on pedestals, we allow them to take the place of God. When they fail us, disillusionment sets in.

Recall an experience you've had with disillusionment, whether it was rooted in mistreatment, abandonment, or other hurts. How did it make you feel to realize that a person or group couldn't live up to your trust?

———————————————————————————————————

———————————————————————————————————

———————————————————————————————————

When you recall the situation today, is your attitude positive or negative?

_____

_____

_____

As you retrace these events, where was God? Can you look back on this situation and see evidence of His presence with you? If not, could it be that you are holding on to resentment that could prevent you from being sensitive to God's presence?

_____

_____

_____

Next, *the cure for disillusionment is putting our hope and trust in the living Lord.* Surely in the darkness of that prison cell, Joseph must have shaken his fist in anger and cried tears of loneliness and loss. Yet his anger did not last because his trust was ultimately in the Lord.

God knows just the right message to give you at just the right time—no matter what dungeon you're in. All it takes is a sensitive heart—not one preoccupied with revenge, bitterness, hostility, or getting even, but one that says, *Lord God, help me now. Deliver me from my own prison. Take the scars that I have experienced and turn them around so I can see Your hand at work. Help me to see You in this abandonment, mistreatment, or rejection.*

Read Psalm 139:7–12. Take a few moments to sit quietly and reflect on these verses, recognizing God's presence in your life. Then write a brief prayer, thanking God for His provision and committing to trust Him for your future.

⚜

Everything can be taken from us except for one precious freedom—the freedom to choose our attitude. With God on our side, all the mistreatment the world has to offer cannot reduce our hope to the ashes of disillusionment. In fact, He may use our positive and godly attitude as a light to shine into the lives of others, maybe even providing a means of escape from our own pit of despair. As Holocaust victim Betsie ten Boom said, "There is no pit so deep that He is not deeper still."[2]

REMEMBERED AND PROMOTED

Genesis 41:1–46

THE HEART OF THE MATTER

Affliction, mistreatment, persecution, hardship, and pain often characterize the Christian walk (1 Peter 4:12). But sometimes God rescues us from our plight, bringing us into new circumstances. For thirteen years Joseph was a slave in Egypt. His family gave him up for dead. He suffered insult and injury. But God was faithful; He never abandoned Joseph. All the while, His plans were in motion, leading Joseph to his release from prison and an unexpected blessing. Through Joseph's example, we can be encouraged to trust God—even in difficult times of waiting.

DISCOVERING THE WAY

When life seems hopeless, it's the promises of God that most often resonate in our hearts, offering hope. Job, a man of affliction if there ever was one, struggled with the questions "Why?" and "How long?" as he faced the physical, emotional, and mental anguish brought on by Satan (Job 1:12). He ached for a chance to plead his innocence before the heavenly Judge. Certainly God would hear his case, if only Job could find Him (23:3–9). But in the midst of his dark night of suffering, Job recalled a divine promise: God "knows the way I take; / When He has tried me, I shall come forth as gold" (23:10). Job was referring to the practice of purifying gold through fire, where impurities (dross) rise to the top and are removed. The longer the fiery process, the purer the gold.

Job knew God was still present. He knew it would take time to refine, to purify, to perfect his character. And for that he would have to wait on the Lord.

DIGGING DEEPER
The Source of Blessing

"God wants your life to be easy; He wants you to enjoy health and wealth right now. Prosperity, after all, is a sign of your faithfulness and of God's unique favor. . . ."

. . . So say many preachers today.

Then why is life so hard? Why do Christians struggle with illness, financial difficulties, broken relationships, and more? The pat answer by the hucksters of prosperity preaching is to blame it on our own lack of faith. But if God's plan is to make our lives easy, then someone forgot to tell Jesus! No one was more faithful to the will of God than Christ (Luke 22:42). And no one experienced suffering like He did (Luke 23).

Don't be deceived. God will not be reduced to a dispenser of pills and bills. He is the sovereign Creator and King of the universe, and He can do as He pleases (Isaiah 45:9; 64:8). He may choose to reward His children with large bank accounts, business successes, or some other material blessings, but *He is under no obligation*. On the other hand, our world is a fallen, sinful place. God may allow His children to live in poverty, to deal with illness, or to suffer persecution as His own Son did. Regardless, we are to remain faithful. We can trust that His ultimate plan for our lives is in motion. And He has promised that His mercy and grace will sustain us (1 Peter 4:19).

The gold Job spoke of was not external rewards—not wealth, not health, not promotions, not renewed and repaired relationships. No. The gold God produces in our lives is depth of character, godly wisdom, purity, and Christlikeness.

Therefore, we shouldn't consider trials and afflictions as intruders, resisting them. Rather, we should submit to God as we go through them and allow Him to refine our character until we come forth as gold.

Job compared character development with something people in his day could easily relate to and visualize — the process of refining gold. Brainstorm to come up with some contemporary metaphors that would make the process of character building relevant to people today. Choose one image, and draw it in the space below.

Somewhere in your drawing above, write the following elements of godly character: *simplicity, silence/solitude, surrender, prayer, humility, self-control, sacrifice.*

Read 1 Peter 5:6–10. Many of the qualities of godly character are mentioned in these verses. Whether you are in a period of waiting right now or have been in the past, ask God to help you see the reason behind the waiting. Ask Him to show you His work in your character as you consider the exercise and answer the following questions.

In your life, what needs perfecting? What is lacking in your character that you want Him to develop?

_____

_____

What needs confirmation? Like setting a bone, what is broken and needs mending?

_____

_____

What needs strengthening? Where are you timid but need to be lion-hearted?

_____

_____

What needs to be established? What aspects of your character need deeper roots or a firmer foundation?

_____

_____

THE TEST: DARKNESS BEFORE DAWN

The great Christian thinker A. W. Tozer has written what must be some of the most difficult words for us to read: "It is doubtful whether God can bless a man greatly until He has hurt him deeply."[1] These words form an appropriate backdrop for what happened in Joseph's life.

Read Genesis 40:23–41:1.

When the cupbearer returned to his trusted position, he immediately forgot about Joseph (Genesis 40:23). For two years Joseph
waited in prison, hoping the cupbearer would mention him to
Pharaoh (41:1).

What was happening during those two years? Nothing. That's
right, nothing . . . at least on the surface. The day the cupbearer was
released from prison Joseph must have sat on the edge of his bed in
expectation, waiting for a pardon to come. And he continued to wait
as hours turned into days, days into months, and months into years.

**Have you experienced a long period of waiting where nothing
seems to happen . . . or at least not quickly enough? What
thoughts go through your mind when you find yourself in this
situation? How do you feel about your circumstances? About
yourself? About God?**

_____

_____

_____

_____

_____

_____

THE TURNING POINT: PHARAOH'S DREAM

More than seven hundred mornings and evenings had come and
gone since the day Joseph interpreted the cupbearer's dream. And
this morning dawned with no more promise than those before. But
unbeknownst to him, on this day his life would be changed forever.
Ironically, the change came about as the result of another dream.

Read Genesis 41:1–13.

As Joseph awoke to face another monotonous day, Pharaoh awoke with his mind reeling over two dreams. In his first dream he saw seven fat, sleek cows coming up out of the Nile River, followed by seven gaunt, ugly cows that devoured the fat ones. He then dreamed of seven plump, good ears of grain growing on a single stalk consumed by seven thin, scorched ears (Genesis 41:1–7). Troubled by this, Pharaoh called for his magicians and wise men to interpret the dreams. But none of them understood the meaning of the dreams (41:8). While the magicians scratched their heads and chins, the cupbearer suddenly—finally—remembered another interpreter of dreams, a young Hebrew man in prison (41:9–13).

 Read Genesis 41:14–32.

Pharaoh wasted no time—he immediately called for Joseph to be brought to him. Pulled from the dungeon, he was cleaned up with a shave and a change of clothes and brought before Pharaoh (Genesis 41:14).

This was Joseph's opportunity—his chance to make the cupbearer look bad in front of his boss and to argue his own innocence before Pharaoh. He did neither. Joseph didn't speak one word of resentment against the cupbearer. He didn't utter a peep about the injustice of his imprisonment. Why? Because Joseph kept his eyes on the Lord, not on his situation.

Pharaoh said to Joseph, "I have heard it said . . . that when you hear a dream you can interpret it" (41:15). Joseph respectfully corrected Pharaoh: "I cannot do it" (41:16 NIV), but God can.

The years of suffering purged Joseph, and he came forth as gold—with the kind of character that refused to use God's gift of interpreting dreams as a bargaining chip to secure his freedom.

Believing he had found a man of understanding, Pharaoh repeated his dream for Joseph (41:17–24). Joseph explained that the seven fat cows and the seven plump ears of grain each represented seven years of great abundance throughout Egypt. This bumper crop would be followed by seven years of famine, as represented by the seven lean cows and thin grain. The intensity of the famine would be so great the people would forget the days of plenty (41:25–31). And the repetition of the dream confirmed the truth and timeliness of the message (41:32).

Throughout the interpretation, Joseph sought to keep Pharaoh's attention on the Lord. List the verses in Genesis 41:14–25 in which Joseph spoke of God.

_____

_____

_____

_____

_____

 Read Genesis 41:33–36.

Because the years of abundance were coming soon, to be followed by the years of famine, Joseph provided Pharaoh with a food distribution plan to save the Egyptian empire from ruin.

For the plan to succeed, Pharaoh would need a man of discernment and wisdom to execute it (Genesis 41:33). But he would have to act quickly and appoint overseers to save and store a portion of the food during the seven good years. During the seven bad years, they would guard and distribute the food (41:34–36).

THE REWARD: JOSEPH'S PROMOTION

Not once did Joseph ask for the job of overseer. Not once did he seek his freedom. Not once did he even mention the injustice done to him. Joseph spoke directly, honestly, and for the glory of God. Though the young Hebrew never placed himself among the "discerning and wise" (Genesis 41:33), Pharaoh clearly saw his insight and skill.

 Read Genesis 41:37–46.

After listening to the interpretation of his dreams and the proposal for how to rescue Egypt, Pharaoh recognized Joseph's God-given qualities, the very ones needed to oversee the task of saving, storing, and distributing food (Genesis 41:37–39).

Then, in one immediate, unexpected, and unsolicited move, Pharaoh promoted Joseph to be overseer of the food distribution program as well as prime minister over the entire land of Egypt (41:40–46). Within the span of a few short moments, Joseph literally went from the pit to the pinnacle.

As you think about Joseph's life thus far, what aspects of his character do you admire the most? Why?

_____

_____

_____

What are some simple ways you can begin to incorporate aspects of these traits into your own life?

_____

_____

_____

STARTING YOUR JOURNEY

Joseph's promotion was incredible. But let's not end our study focusing on the signet ring and gold necklace he wore and forget the gold character it adorned. His character reveals two important lessons for us to learn.

First, *during the waiting period, trust God without panic.* We must learn to trust God to handle the cupbearers in our lives—the ones who forget us, who reject us, who break their promises. God will take care of the cupbearers. Our job is to remain faithful as we wait. Others may forget or forsake us, but God never will. He cares enough about us to use waiting to build our character.

Trusting God is often difficult, especially during times of waiting or when others hurt us. For encouragement, read Philippians 4:6–7 and answer the following questions.

What are we *not* to do?

_____

What are we supposed to do?

_____

_____

What does God promise?

_____

Second, *during the time of reward, thank God without pride.* As we wait during the dungeon times of life, pride is slowly stripped away. While sitting there, we often ask God for endurance and promise to thank Him and glorify Him once we are released. But when the cell door is flung open, the temptation is to forget the suffering and waiting and to believe we deserve the good that is now coming to us. We must resist that temptation, consistently and humbly thanking God for His blessing.

Jacob, Joseph's father, had a practical solution to remind himself to praise God in times of blessing. Read Genesis 33:18–20 and 35:7, 14–15. What did Jacob do?

_____

_____

_____

What are some physical reminders you can develop to help you remember God's goodness to you during times of waiting? How might you thank Him for the character qualities He developed in your life during that time?

_____

_____

_____

⚘

Pride, rebellion, self-sufficiency . . . the dross of our character is incinerated in the crucible called *waiting*. We tend to do everything we can to avoid this furnace. We engage in mindless distractions or busy work. We complain that the waiting period is useless, wasted time—especially when we see nothing happening. But God is at work refining our character. Don't despair; continue to trust and praise God for the work He is doing and will continue to do.

REAPING THE REWARDS OF RIGHTEOUSNESS

Genesis 41:41–57

THE HEART OF THE MATTER

Christians are notoriously negative. Usually we focus on the difficulties, the pressures, and the problems of walking with God rather than the benefits and blessings of a relationship with Him. And many of us have thought at one time or another that godliness doesn't pay — at least not in tangible ways. When we see Christians prosper, we tend to raise our eyebrows and become suspicious of their faith. It just doesn't seem "spiritual" to be prosperous. But Joseph is an example of a man who was rewarded for his righteousness, and he kept his integrity intact. His story also teaches us how we should respond to Christians whom God prospers.

DISCOVERING THE WAY

Before we begin our study, let's take a little test.

On a scale of one to five, how helpful and encouraging are you when other people are going through tough times?

Not Affirming   Very Affirming
1   2   3   4   5

How encouraging and affirming are you when someone is suddenly promoted and becomes more prosperous?

Not Affirming   Very Affirming
1   2   3   4   5

Did you respond differently to the second question? When we see someone who is prosperous, we often become critical rather than joyful, suspicious rather than supportive. As a result, we're more supportive of those with humble means than of people with abundant means.

When you see someone who is very wealthy or successful and then find out that person is a Christian, are you just a little bit skeptical of that person's faith, of his or her depth as a believer? Be honest.

_____

_____

_____

Why do you think people often equate suffering with spirituality and prosperity with carnality?

_____

_____

_____

If Joseph were a Christian friend of ours, he and his family would be on our prayer list. We would dispatch pastors and counselors to comfort his grief-stricken father. We would provide meals for his family. We might even collect new and gently used clothes for him or send a Bible to his prison cell.

Praying and comforting would seem like the least we could do for a friend who has gone through the difficulties Joseph endured. His brothers hated him. They stole his favorite coat, threw him into a well, and sold him as a slave. He was forced to learn a new language and a new culture. His master was kind enough, but the lady of the house tried to seduce him—repeatedly. She then accused him of attempted rape, which landed him in prison where he was forgotten for two years by a friend who also neglected to ask for his pardon.

A MAN RESTORED

In the final seventeen verses of Genesis 41, our prayers for Joseph are answered. But would we continue to pray for our friend after he was suddenly promoted to a position of power? Or would we point a bony finger and warn him: "Not every man can carry a full cup. Sudden elevation frequently leads to pride and a fall. . . . [T]he most exacting test of all [is] prosperity"? [1]

Though prosperity is usually a blessing, it can also be a difficult test of a person's integrity. Summarize each of the following Scriptures in your own words, and note what they say regarding prosperity.

Proverbs 23:4–5

_____

_____

Matthew 6:24

_____

_____

Hebrews 13:5

_____

_____

In your own experience, how have Christians you have known or have observed handled prosperity? Give a few brief examples, both positive and negative.

_____

_____

_____

Why do you think it is so often difficult to handle prosperity with integrity? Be specific.

_____

_____

_____

You'll remember from the previous lesson that Pharaoh retrieved Joseph from prison for him to interpret Pharaoh's dreams. Along with the interpretation, Joseph laid out a plan to save the Egyptian people from starvation during the coming famine. Recognizing Joseph's divine gifts of discernment and wisdom, Pharaoh immediately promoted him from prisoner to prime minister, giving him absolute authority over all of Egypt.

NEW AUTHORITY

In addition to having food during the famine, the perks of Joseph's new role included a position of great authority, a new name, and a new wife and family. His position offered him three levels of new-found authority.

 Read Genesis 41:41–45.

Joseph was given territorial authority (Genesis 41:41). The whole country lay before him, under his control. Egypt was a land richly nourished by the Nile, covered with cities and stately temples, with ports and trade routes bringing commerce and wealth.

Pharaoh also gave Joseph limitless financial authority (41:42). The term _signet ring_ comes from the Hebrew verb meaning "to sink down."[2] The ring was used to deeply imprint Pharaoh's "signature" into soft clay. Joseph could now buy anything he wished. Along with the signet ring, he was also given additional jewelry and a new wardrobe made of "fine linen."

As if that weren't enough, Joseph was given public authority. Pharaoh gave Joseph a government-issued chariot and bodyguards who commanded the public to bow as he passed by (41:43). Pharaoh then proclaimed that, next to himself, Joseph was the most powerful man in Egypt (41:44).

Wow! What a meteoric rise.

In your own words, define prosperity. What is your attitude toward individuals whose lives possess those characteristics? Be candid.

_____

_____

_____

Glance back over Genesis 41:41–44. What is Joseph saying or doing?

_____

_____

_____

What can we learn from Joseph's silence about how to handle promotion and prosperity?

_____

_____

_____

 Read Genesis 41:45–49.

Joseph had it all, or so it seemed. But it is likely that his Hebrew name caused some suspicion to grow in the minds of the average Egyptians, no matter how low they bowed to the ground. So Pharaoh gave Joseph a new name — Zaphenath-paneah (Genesis 41:45).

GETTING TO THE ROOT
A New Name

Ancient names were usually selected not because the parents favored a particular name, but because names held meaning. Often they memorialized an important event or revealed something about the person's character. For example, *Yoseph* (Joseph) is closely linked to two Hebrew verbs: *'asaf* and *yosef*—"to take away" and "to add." [3] At Joseph's birth, Rachel declared, "God has taken away my reproach" (Genesis 30:23). Then she prayed, "May [YAHWEH] give me another son" (30:24).

Renaming was equally significant, and it was common practice (Genesis 17:3–5, 15; 32:27–28; Daniel 1:7; Matthew 16:17–18; Acts 13:9). For Joseph, his new name, Zaphenath-paneah, was an attempt to "Egyptianize" him. [4] Joseph's name may have reflected his ability to interpret dreams; he was a "revealer of secrets." [5] Literally, Zaphenath-paneah is translated, "the god speaks and he lives," from the root word *nath*. [6] In his way of thinking, Pharaoh may have been honoring the Egyptian goddess Neith for giving Joseph the ability to interpret dreams.

Interestingly, the Bible never refers to Joseph as Zaphenath-paneah again.

A New Wife

Joseph would have never rejected his Hebrew name and selected this Egyptian name, but he didn't have a say in the matter. Nor did he have a say about whom he would marry: "And [Pharaoh] gave him Asenath, the daughter of Potiphera priest of On" (Genesis 41:45). Her name also includes the root word *nath*, and it means "belongs to (the goddess) Neith." [7] We're not told whether she was bright or dull, beautiful or ugly, sympathetic to Joseph's faith or antagonistic—only that she was the daughter of an Egyptian priest.

A new position, a new name, a new wife. Joseph was only 30 years old, a young man with a bright future. And for the next seven years he traveled throughout the country setting up a process of storing and distributing the abundance of grain in Egypt, which flowed in "like the sand of the sea . . . beyond measure" (41:49).

If Joseph were on your prayer list, would you still be praying for him like you did when he was in prison? Would you still be supportive of this well-dressed young man as he passed by with his entourage? What about that new name—it's so worldly—would it give you pause? Or how about his wife, the daughter of a pagan priest? Would she be disturbing to your sensibilities? Would you be skeptical that Joseph was compromising his faith to get rich?

Sometimes we're defeated by our own attitudes about money, prosperity, and God's sense of fairness. What do the following verses say about the wisdom and source of all blessing?

1 Chronicles 29:11–12

_____

Psalm 115:1–3; 135:6

_____

Proverbs 30:8–9

_____

BLESSING DURING FAMINE

We have noted Joseph's newfound outward power and prestige, but can we tell what's going on in his heart?

 Read Genesis 41:50–52.

In naming his sons, Joseph used a play on words, revealing his true nature. We shouldn't overlook the obvious—he gave his boys Hebrew names. And more importantly, their names commemorated God's provision, revealing Joseph's continued hope and trust in the Lord.

The name of Joseph's first born was Manasseh. At the root of his name is *nashah*, meaning "to forget."[8] The Hebrew construction means "to take the sting out of a memory." Literally, Joseph said, "God [Manasseh-ed me]"; "God has made me forget all my trouble and all my father's household" (Genesis 41:51).

The name of his second son was Ephraim. This name comes from the verb meaning "to be fruitful."[9] He was a living reminder of how God had "Ephraim-ed" Joseph—making him fruitful in the land of his affliction (41:52).

Underneath the exterior trappings of Egyptian royalty beat a heart that was still committed to worshiping God.

 Read Genesis 41:53–57.

When the famine hit, Joseph didn't go hungry (Genesis 41:53–54). And he never took advantage of his royal position, nor did he compromise his integrity.

When the people begged Pharaoh to fill their empty bellies, Pharaoh sent them to Joseph (41:55). What did Joseph do? He opened the great storehouses and sold grain to the hungry Egyptians and to people from surrounding lands, because the famine was worldwide (41:56–57).

STARTING YOUR JOURNEY

Would it be more difficult to identify with Joseph once he looked a lot different from the poor prisoner? A lot different from you? Or even a lot different from the average celebrity? If we got to know him, we would see that, though Joseph had the trappings of high office, he wasn't pompous, and he didn't abuse his authority.

As we consider Joseph's past, we can make several important observations about his integrity and godly character.

Lengthy affliction did not discourage Joseph. Joseph was thrown into a pit, sold as a slave, and put into prison. He endured thirteen years of unrelenting hardship! Imagine the emotional and physical anguish of those events. And yet, Joseph didn't allow discouragement to imprison his heart. He maintained his hope by focusing on God and committing his life to Him.

And *Joseph's bad memories did not defeat him.* Joseph was the ideal candidate for bitterness. He carried with him the memories of brothers who hated him, of an immoral woman who ruined his reputation, of a supposed friend who forgot about him. But Joseph didn't let these memories keep him in the pit of despair and anger.

Remember, these factors are often present in the lives of modern-day "Josephs" as well. Many have wrestled with discouragement and bitter memories and remained committed to God. Christians who are wealthy by the world's standards may be wealthy by God's standards as well. So, *great blessings need not disqualify.*

Rather than distance ourselves from them, we should thank God for the "Josephs" in our generation. We should help these believers use their authority and success for His glory. Perhaps, if we were more affirming and supportive, fewer would stumble and fall.

Look back over your affirmation scales in this chapter. Overall, how affirming are you toward the "Josephs" in your life?

Not Affirming				Very Affirming
1	2	3	4	5

What can you do to encourage and affirm one of the "Josephs" in your life? How might you pray for that person?

_____

_____

_____

If you're currently a "Joseph," what specific measures are you putting in place to ensure that you will remain humble and grateful to God during this time?

It's hard to be supportive of those who've received outward blessings from the Lord, especially while you're enduring affliction. It's almost impossible to do so if you're nursing painful memories. But neither of these situations should discourage us from affirming those who prosper. Remember, it's the Lord who "Manasseh-s" and "Ephraim-s" us.

LESSON SIX

ACTIVATING A SEARED CONSCIENCE
Genesis 42:1–28

THE HEART OF THE MATTER

Are you the type of person who remembers what you ought to forget and forgets what you ought to remember? Think about that provocative question for a moment. Joseph had many years to ponder his answer. After seven years of blessing and abundance, the famine was in full bloom. People from the surrounding lands were coming to Egypt for grain — including Joseph's brothers. Upon recognizing the men who threw him into a pit and sold him as a slave, Joseph faced a difficult decision. Should he review his mental blacklist or shred it? Should he punish or forgive? Would Joseph be the type of person who remembers what he ought to forget and forgets what he ought to remember? Are you?

DISCOVERING THE WAY

After thirteen years as a pauper, Joseph now prospered in Egypt. But what of his family? How were they faring? Were his brothers taking care of their aging father? Did they think of Joseph? Did they wonder what had become of him? Or did they push him out of their minds? Were their consciences asleep?

Joseph was about to find out.

A FAMINE IN CANAAN

Seven bountiful years brought Egyptian granaries to overflowing (Genesis 41:49). But now, few crops grew in the baked soil, and what managed to break through was burned up under the scorching sun.

55

The long-predicted famine had arrived, and it had two important qualities. It was *widespread*, not limited (41:54, 56–57), and it was *severe*, not slight (41:55–57).

 Read Genesis 42:1–5.

Sweeping out of Egypt and into surrounding areas, the cruelty of the famine reached Canaan, stealing food from the mouths of Joseph's father, Jacob, and his family. The old man scolded his sons for standing around looking dumb. "Why are you staring at one another? . . . I have heard that there is grain in Egypt; go down there and buy some for us" (Genesis 42:1–2). Didn't they understand that starvation was a matter of life and death?

Getting the message, ten of Jacob's sons packed their bags and left, leaving Benjamin behind because Jacob was worried something might happen to him on the journey (42:3–5).

Read Genesis 35:16–19 and 42:4. Based on what you've learned in this study so far, why do you think Jacob kept "Joseph's brother" (42:4) from the journey? Why was Benjamin so important to Jacob?

_____

_____

_____

As we follow the path of Jacob's sons, keep in mind that neither they nor Jacob knew what had become of Joseph. In fact, he probably didn't even cross their minds. They only had one assignment: bring back groceries. Sitting in his plush office in Egypt, Joseph had no idea that his brothers—the very ones who sold him into slavery—were on their way to buy grain from him. Their encounter would change their lives forever.

AN ENCOUNTER IN EGYPT

Egypt had become the soup kitchen for a starving world. Each week, thousands of hungry people stood in line, waiting to buy food from the wise prime minister who had shrewdly prepared for the seven-year famine.

 Read Genesis 42:6–8.

Joseph's day began like any other day, looking into the gaunt faces of foreigners. Bowing and then standing before him were bearded men, clad in Hebrew garb—not unlike others he certainly saw regularly—but these men were different (Genesis 42:6). They were his brothers.

He recognized them, but why didn't they recognize him? It had been more than twenty years since the brothers had last seen Joseph, and he was just a boy of seventeen then. While the Hebrews usually wore rough, handwoven clothing and maintained full beards, Joseph was clean-shaven and wore Egyptian linen. He spoke Egyptian as if it were his native language. Even if the brothers had anticipated the remote possibility of seeing Joseph, they would have been searching the faces of Hebrew slaves, not those of the Egyptian rulers. And the Scripture points out that Joseph "spoke to them harshly" (42:7). No wonder they didn't recognize him (42:8)!

 Read Genesis 42:9–12.

The shock of suddenly seeing his brothers jolted Joseph's memory. As a youth, he had dreamed of sheaves of grain and stars bowing before him (Genesis 37:6–7, 9). Now, after more than two decades, his dreams were coming true.

As his brothers bowed before him, questions must have raced through his mind. What of Benjamin? What of Jacob? But then, painful memories may have begun to surface one by one . . . accusing faces, the darkness of an earthen pit, the whip of the slave trader. Somehow Joseph had to find out, without revealing who he was, whether they still hated him, whether they felt any sorrow or guilt over what they had done. In a test of their motives and character, he accused them of being spies (42:9).

Do you have a mental "blacklist" of people who have hurt you, lied about you, or rejected you? Have you ever encountered one of these people unexpectedly? If so, what memories did that person trigger?

_____

_____

_____

How did you treat that person?

_____

_____

_____

If you were to encounter this person again, would you treat him or her differently? Why?

_____

_____

_____

 Read Genesis 42:13–17.

With Joseph's unrelenting finger pointing directly at them, the brothers pled their innocence. They were ten of twelve sons, all born to one father who was living in Canaan. The youngest was still with his father, and "one is no longer alive" (Genesis 42:13). Joseph might as well have been dead; he was buried and forgotten in their hearts and minds. Their consciences were seared—the tears he cried and the anguish he suffered were merely memories.

Joseph repeated his indictment: "you are spies." But to test their truthfulness, he instructed them to send one brother back to fetch Benjamin while the others remained under guard in Egypt. The words barely escaped Joseph's mouth before he got carried away in the emotion of the moment, forgot his original plan, and promptly threw all of them into prison (42:14–17).

Why do you think Joseph based the test of their truthfulness on bringing Benjamin to Egypt?

_____

_____

_____

Commentator F. B. Meyer makes some insightful observations about Joseph's encounter with his brothers.

> In all this, I believe [Joseph] *repeated exactly the scene at the pit's mouth.* . . . It is not unlikely that when they saw him coming toward them, in his prince-like dress, they had rushed at him, accusing him of having come to spy out their corrupt behavior, and take back an evil report to their father, as he had done before. If so, this will explain why he now suddenly accused them of being spies. No doubt the lad protested that he was no spy . . . but they had met his protestations with rude violence in much the same way as the rough-speaking governor now treated them. . . . If this were the case — and it seems most credible — it is obvious that it was a powerful appeal to their conscience and memory, and one that could not fail to awaken both.[1]

The brothers sat in a dungeon for three days. What happened during that time? It obviously gave them time to think — and time for God to awaken their consciences.

And what of Joseph; what was he doing those three days? He was devising a plan.

Read Genesis 42:18–23.

Instead of sending one brother back to Canaan and keeping the rest, Joseph ordered all to return except one. Their assignment this time: bring back Benjamin (Genesis 42:18–20).

While packing, the brothers had a conversation in Hebrew. Thinking the prime minister couldn't understand, they confessed their sin against their brother Joseph. Their seared consciences began to revive (42:21–23).

The original language helps us fully appreciate their admission of guilt. In Hebrew, "we" is in the emphatic position: *"we* are guilty"; *"we* saw the distress of his soul"; *"we* would not listen." They didn't blame the passivity of Jacob. They didn't blame the teenage pride of Joseph. They blamed themselves.

Deeply remorseful, they remembered the distress of Joseph when they sold him into slavery. Now, that same soulful anguish, that same emotional and spiritual bondage, shackled their hearts.

Think of a time when you knowingly wronged someone. Did you ever fully come to grips with your sin? How did that make you feel?

_____

_____

_____

What effect did this sin have on your relationship with that person? On your walk with the Lord?

_____

_____

_____

Read Genesis 42:24–28.

Hearing their confession and seeing their distress, Joseph was overcome with emotion and had to leave the room for fear of giving away his identity. Composing himself, he returned and placed Simeon in shackles (Genesis 42:24).

Just before the nine brothers set out on their journey, Joseph secretly performed an act of grace. He filled their bags with grain, fulfilling the original purpose of their visit. He gave them provisions for the journey, which was a cultural courtesy. And he returned their money (42:25).

Summarize in your own words what the following passages teach us about how God desires us to treat an enemy.

Luke 6:27–31, 35

_____

_____

_____

Romans 12:14, 17–21

_____

_____

_____

Write out a specific plan of action to apply the truth in these Scriptures in your dealings with those on your "blacklist." For example, whom do you need to love? What does "turning the other cheek" look like? Be practical.

_____

_____

_____

After writing what you will do, stop and ask the Lord to give you an opportunity and the grace to carry out your plan, as well as the wisdom to modify it when necessary.

At their first stop, one of the brothers opened his sack to feed his donkey and discovered the money. Staring at each other, "their hearts sank," and the brothers began to tremble. Then they asked a penetrating question—the kind usually raised by people whose consciences have been awakened: "What is this that God has done to us?" (Genesis 42:28). Finally, they began to sense God's hand in these strange events.

 STARTING YOUR JOURNEY
Though most of us would hate to admit it, we usually act more like the brothers than like Joseph. But just as God awakened the consciences of these brothers, so God can rouse our own.

First, *God activates our seared consciences when we're victims of unfair treatment similar to what we once gave someone else.* Joseph accused the brothers of being spies. He threw them into prison. And he kept one from returning home. Each of these events was similar to what Joseph experienced. And the soulful distress they experienced reminded them of Joseph and began to stir their consciences.

Have you ever treated someone unfairly and later received similar treatment from someone else? What happened?

_____

_____

_____

What thoughts and feelings did you experience during this time? How did you respond?

_____

_____

_____

Second, *God activates our seared consciences when we're recipients of undeserved expressions of grace.* As the prime minister of Egypt, Joseph could have given his brothers what they deserved—slavery and imprisonment. Instead, they received grain, money, and freedom. It was this act of grace that finally roused their sleeping consciences.

Briefly describe a time when you deserved punishment or rebuke but received grace instead.

_____

_____

_____

Read Romans 5:6–8 and Ephesians 1:7–8. In your own words, summarize what these verses say about grace.

_____

_____

_____

In light of the grace God has given you through His Son, Jesus Christ, how should you respond to someone who wrongs you?

_____

_____

_____

Are you the type of person who remembers what you ought to forget and forgets what you ought to remember? Do you have a blacklist of those who've hurt you, lied about you, or rejected you? If so, shred your list before you get a hardened conscience, develop a thick and calloused soul, and grow insensitive to God. Commit yourself to showing love and extending grace. Leave "the brothers" in your life to the Lord.

GROANINGS OF A SAD DAD

Genesis 42:29–43:15

THE HEART OF THE MATTER

Have you ever accidentally dropped an open-faced peanut butter and jelly sandwich? In that split second before impact, your eyes widen with both childlike optimism and horror. You hope against hope that maybe, despite gravity and Murphy's Law, your little sandwich will be the miracle sandwich that lands right-side up. Maybe, oh just maybe . . . *splat!* Much of Jacob's life was just like that—peanut-butter-and-jelly-side-down. Though seasoned in walking with God, he remained a victim of his own carnal clumsiness. Instead of seeing the Lord's hand of protection on his sons' lives, he became paralyzed by fear, worry, and resentment. Jacob relied on himself rather than on God's strength. And his reluctance to trust God almost led to disaster. Sometimes we tend to be just like Jacob—expecting the worst rather than trusting God's best.

DISCOVERING THE WAY

We all have days when an inexorable force seems to be thwarting and frustrating our every move. We wash the car and it rains. We make a sandwich, turn around for a moment, and suddenly the plate is empty, the dog licking his chops. Stuff happens—and it's often out of our control. But we *can* control our response to it.

65

OUR NATURAL TENDENCIES

When we experience multiple, consecutive P-B-J-side-down days, it can feel like the world is against us. We often become defensive, closed-minded, and suspicious, following a three-step pattern that's deeply rooted in human nature.

First, we tend to respond *negatively* rather than *positively*.

Do you tend to agree or disagree with sayings like the ones below? Why? How often do you find yourself thinking these or similar thoughts?

- **"No good deed goes unpunished."**

- **"If you're feeling good, don't worry; you'll get over it."**

- **"Anything that can go wrong will go wrong."**

Second, we tend to view problems *horizontally*, from a strictly human perspective, rather than *vertically*, from a godly perspective. If we do shift to a vertical view, it's usually *after* we've made things worse by trying to solve the problem ourselves.

Third, we tend to *resist* what is new rather than *accept* it—especially if it seems to offer something for nothing. "There's no such thing as a free lunch," we're told. So we remain suspicious of anything that sounds too good to be true—that doesn't carry a price tag in plain view.

Read Ephesians 2:8–9. What does Paul say about salvation?

_____

_____

_____

Using John 3:16, Romans 6:23, Ephesians 1:5–8, and
Ephesians 2:8–9, how could you convince someone who doesn't
believe in "free lunches" that salvation in Christ is a free gift?
(For help with your answer, see "How to Begin a Relationship
with God" at the end of this Bible Companion.)

_____

_____

_____

If they're not dealt with, these natural tendencies will grow
stronger as we get older. Jacob could testify to that. Even though
he walked with God for well over a hundred years, he constantly
undermined his faith by his negativism, horizontal thinking, and
closed-mindedness.

JACOB'S INITIAL RESISTANCE AND RELUCTANCE

Back in Jacob's tent, nine sons had returned safely from buying
grain in Egypt. But what should have been a happy occasion instead
became morose.

 Read Genesis 42:29–34.

As the boys unloaded their donkeys and shook the dust from
their robes, Jacob must have been counting noses. *One, two, three . . .
seven, eight, nine. . . . One is missing—Simeon. Where's Simeon?* Sitting
Jacob down, the brothers explained what had happened in Egypt
(Genesis 42:29–34).

What two important details did the sons leave out of their report? See Genesis 42:17, 27 for a hint.

_____

_____

_____

Why do you think they failed to mention these facts?

_____

_____

_____

We don't know what Jacob was thinking while listening to this tale, but it's clear from the next verses that he assumed the worst.

 Read Genesis 42:35–38.

Pouring out their grain, the brothers made a startling discovery—bundles of money tumbled out of each of their sacks. What a wonderful provision from the Lord! But did the brothers, or the father for that matter, praise God? Hardly. They were afraid (Genesis 42:35).

Immediately, Jacob's fear ran roughshod over his senses. He blamed his sons for the loss of Joseph and Simeon, and he became distressed that they wanted to take Benjamin (42:36). But Jacob was jumping to conclusions. The brothers didn't say Simeon was *dead*—he was actually in an Egyptian prison (42:19).

If Jacob had slowed down to ponder the situation, perhaps he could have discerned the Lord's hand. But he didn't.

Ever heard the old saying, "You're not paranoid if everyone really is out to get you"? Describe a time when you jumped to a conclusion or felt paranoid about a situation. Did your assumption turn out to be right or wrong?

_____

_____

_____

How did your assumption affect your relationships?

_____

_____

_____

How did your assumption affect your walk with Christ?

_____

_____

_____

Reuben, the oldest son, sensing that Jacob was utterly resistant to letting Benjamin go, made a last-ditch appeal (Genesis 42:37–38). But Jacob flatly refused! Benjamin was all he had left from his beloved Rachel. He called him "my son," not their brother (42:38). Jacob couldn't entertain the thought that Benjamin might be harmed. His final answer was no . . . or so he thought.

JACOB'S FINAL ACCEPTANCE

Changing Jacob's stubborn heart was no quick and easy task. But continued hardship has a way of peeling back the layers of our resistance.

Read Genesis 43:1–5.

Jacob's first layer of resistance was denial and delay. He did not act immediately. He and his family took their time eating the grain the brothers had brought from Egypt. But the famine, which had already consumed their crops, lingered on (Genesis 43:1). The cupboard was bare once again. So, Jacob came up with a brilliant plan: "Go back, buy us a little food" (43:2). Go back? How could they go back? Jacob was in complete denial. The brothers couldn't go back without Benjamin. Judah reminded Jacob of that cold, hard truth. "Read my lips, Dad," you can almost hear him say in exasperation. Then Judah repeated what Joseph had said: "You will not see my face unless your brother is with you" (Genesis 43:5). Period. End of discussion.

 Read Genesis 43:6–10.

His next layer was blame and deceit. Jacob blamed his sons for being honest! Why couldn't they have just lied about having another brother (43:6)? We see that mixed into Jacob's "Murphy's Law mentality" was a willingness to be deceitful when cornered.

 DIGGING DEEPER
From Jacob to Israel
Jacob was renamed "Israel," meaning "God strives," after he wrestled with God (Genesis 32:22–32). But as the biblical narrative continues, he is still referred to as "Jacob." So why does the text in Genesis 43 suddenly begin calling him "Israel"? The name "Jacob" represents the patriarch's humanity, while "Israel" reveals his headship over God's chosen people. Though we see his suffering in Genesis 43, the primary focus of this passage is on his official role of instructing his sons and committing them to the care of El Shaddai.[1]

Finally, Judah proposed a plan: he would trade his life for Benjamin's if anything were to happen to him (43:8–9). After all, Judah argued, the delay had already been costly (43:10).

 Read Genesis 43:11–12.

Next, Jacob began to soften, responding with tolerance and uncertainty. He was suspicious, unwilling to consider God's goodness or protection. With a heavy sigh and a grim face, Jacob grudgingly agreed to let Benjamin go. But to ensure his safety, Jacob sent along gifts (Genesis 43:11). He assumed that one can never be too careful in dealing with Egyptian officials. Besides, the same ploy worked against his brother, Esau (32:2–33:11).

Jacob didn't commit Benjamin to the Lord's care, trusting Him to preserve and protect Benjamin's life. Jacob trusted in the feeble hope of a horizontal, human-focused plan, substituting pistachio nuts for prayer; almonds for the Almighty. If these weren't enough, he told them to pay off the prime minister with more money (43:12).

 Read Genesis 43:13–15.

Finally, after exhausting all other possibilities, Jacob submitted to the plan with guarded faith and abandonment. And with the same deep sigh, he loosened his grip on Benjamin and hoped the Lord would extend mercy so that the Egyptian would release his sons (Genesis 43:13–14). Perfunctory though it may be, his prayer shows a glimmer of faith.

Way to go Jacob! Now you're starting to look up. What's that you said? No, don't look down. Don't say it . . . too late. "For me, nothing's left; I've lost everything" (43:14 MSG). Jacob essentially threw up his hands and said, "If none of you come back, I guess I'll just have to live with it." Jacob revealed his negative, horizontal mentality, shallow faith, and unwillingness to trust God fully.

Rate your natural tendencies when faced with difficult and uncertain decisions.

Denial and Delay				Acceptance and Action
1	2	3	4	5

Blame and Deceit				Responsibility and Integrity
1	2	3	4	5

Tolerance and Uncertainty				Joy and Prayer
1	2	3	4	5

Guarded Faith and Grudging Acceptance				Radical Faith and Trust
1	2	3	4	5

Then the brothers, including Benjamin, packed up their things and left for Egypt (43:15).

STARTING YOUR JOURNEY

Perhaps we shouldn't be too hard on Jacob. We've all struggled against the undercurrents of negativism, a horizontal perspective, and resistance to new ideas. But we don't have to go with the flow of our natural tendencies. We can swim upstream, if we learn to cultivate the following three habits.

Recognize and admit your negative mentality. This may sound elementary, but if you're going to major in godly thinking, no matter how smart you are, then confession is the first test you must pass.

What kept you from seeing God's hand in the things that you couldn't handle this week? This month?

_____

_____

_____

Read each of the following passages. What does each one pre-scribe as a remedy for a negative mentality?

Romans 12:2

_____

_____

_____

2 Corinthians 4:16–18

_____

_____

_____

Philippians 4:8–9

_____

_____

_____

1 Thessalonians 5:16–19

_____

_____

_____

Force a vertical, godly focus until it begins to flow. Our natural tendency is to trust in ourselves, to look at life from the horizontal perspective. The longer we stay in this current, the quicker it carries us away. Reversing the flow is difficult, but one good place to begin cultivating a vertical focus is by asking yourself, "What is God trying to say to me in this situation?"

In the chart below, briefly describe the top three challenges in your life right now; then prayerfully fill in the column on the right.

My Challenges	What is God trying to say to me in this situation?
1.	
2.	
3.	

God has provided us with several means for understanding His eternal perspective on our lives. Consider the following passages of Scripture. After each set, note where we can find His instruction or encouragement.

Psalm 119:105 and 2 Timothy 3:16–17

John 14:26 and John 16:13

Proverbs 11:14 and Proverbs 20:18

Stay open to a new idea for at least five minutes. Once you make a hasty decision, your pride will do everything it can to keep you from backing down. Try holding off for five minutes before deciding whether to accept or reject a new idea, perspective, or proposal.

What creative solutions might you apply to the problems you listed in the chart? Having trouble thinking outside the box? To whom could you turn for godly, wise, or even off-the-wall counsel? Write those names below.

_____

_____

_____

As you discuss potential solutions with your advisors, try to stay open-minded. What would be the benefits and drawbacks of each solution? Even if you decide to reject the advice, were you able to consider it for five minutes? Were you able to focus on the possibilities?

_____

_____

_____

Continue to pray about the issue, asking God to help you have a positive mind-set, maintain a vertical focus, and be open to new ideas. Confess your difficulty and commit to trusting His perfect plan for you.

None of us can prevent peanut-butter-and-jelly-side-down days. Not in an upside-down world. But we must learn that it's not just what happens *to* us that makes life hard. It's our natural response to those situations that often makes life harder. But with God's help and a little practice, we don't have to follow our natural tendencies—we can take a positive, vertical, open approach to life!

FEAR DISPLACED BY GRACE

Genesis 43:15–34

THE HEART OF THE MATTER

Philip Yancey called *grace* "the last best word." Grace is "like a vast aquifer," he wrote, "reminding us that good things come not from our own efforts, rather by the grace of God. Even now, despite our secular drift, taproots still stretch towards grace." [1] Modeling God's grace, Joseph welcomed his brothers into his home, responding to their mistreatment of him with kindness and blessing, and gathering into a family those who had long been alienated. And as we watch his shamefaced brothers receive Joseph's outpouring of grace, we will be challenged to set aside our guilt and fear and accept God's free gift of grace.

DISCOVERING THE WAY

Joseph's brothers were well acquainted with guilt and uncertainty. Even though their consciences had been pricked on their recent trip to Egypt, they still hadn't fully repented of their twenty-year-old sin against Joseph. They hoped that their return trip to Egypt would allow them to prove they weren't spies, ransom Simeon, and buy more food.

En Route from Canaan to Egypt

Leaving their father behind, the brothers took along three prized possessions.

 Read Genesis 43:15.

They carried large baskets filled with delicacies of "balm and . . . honey, aromatic gum and myrrh, pistachio nuts and almonds" (Genesis 43:11). They carried double the amount of money to pay for the grain, plus the money that had been returned to them on their last trip. And most importantly, they brought Benjamin.

These were the things they carried outwardly. Inwardly, they carried the heavy baggage of guilt for mistreating Joseph (42:21) and deep-seated anxiety about seeing the Egyptian prime minister again. Would he release Simeon? Would he use the money found in their sacks as an excuse to throw them into the dungeon too?

If you were to imagine what guilt looks like, what picture would you draw or paste here?

Guilt

Because we're all sinners, we've all felt guilty at one time or another. Think of a time when a sin weighed heavy on your conscience. Describe the emotions you felt. Did you finally confess? Why, or why not?

_____

_____

_____

_____

_____

_____

FEARFUL BROTHERS WITH JOSEPH'S BUTLER

One morning Joseph looked out his window and saw ten men approaching, including his beloved brother Benjamin. He immediately ordered a feast, anticipating a reunion with his family.

 Read Genesis 43:16–22.

But something seemed terrifyingly wrong to the brothers. They had expected to meet the prime minister at the public granary, not at his home. Unknowingly illustrating the truth of Shakespeare's words, "Suspicion always haunts the guilty mind," [2] the brothers fretted that this turn of events came about because of the money found in their sacks. Certainly the prime minister would enslave them, along with their donkeys (Genesis 43:18).

Consumed by fear and guilt, they stumbled over each other to provide Joseph's butler with an unnecessary explanation.

What encouragement does each of these passages give for a guilty conscience?

Psalm 32:5

_____

_____

_____

Proverbs 28:13

_____

_____

_____

1 John 1:9

_____

_____

_____

Fear and guilt had eaten away at the brothers' consciences until they were utterly miserable. But, unexpectedly, they were about to receive the first of several gracious gifts.

Forgiveness is an expression of grace, which has been explained as "unmerited favor." If you were to capture an image of grace, what picture would you draw or paste here?

Grace

Describe a time when you experienced grace.

_____

_____

_____

 Read Genesis 43:23–25.

While they were babbling on about the money, the butler broke in and spoke the calming Hebrew word *shalom*, which means "be at peace; calm down; take a deep breath; don't be afraid." And if this weren't enough to put their minds at ease, he began to proclaim God's faithfulness and provision: "Your God . . . the God of your father has given you treasure in your sacks" (Genesis 43:23).

The brothers must have been dumbfounded. An Egyptian speaking Hebrew? And *he* understood what *God* was doing? Barely recovering from the butler's eloquent testimony, the brothers were hit with another shock—Simeon was brought out to them (43:23). Stunned at seeing Simeon looking healthy and well after his time in prison, they received one more surprise. Joseph's butler brought them into the house, and instead of putting shackles on their feet, he extended hospitality by washing their feet, giving them a cool drink of water, and taking care of their donkeys (43:24). They were bewildered!

But they hadn't seen the prime minister yet. What if he didn't share the butler's theology regarding the money? What if he was angry? Still struggling with fear and guilt, the brothers decided to put their presents for Joseph in order (43:25).

When you have offended them, how difficult is it for you to _receive_ grace (blessing, acceptance, favor, or forgiveness—with no strings attached) from the following?

	Easy				Difficult
Stranger	1	2	3	4	5
Friend	1	2	3	4	5
Parents	1	2	3	4	5
In-laws	1	2	3	4	5
Siblings	1	2	3	4	5
Children	1	2	3	4	5
Spouse	1	2	3	4	5

GRATEFUL BROTHERS WITH JOSEPH

Standing in the prime minister's house, waiting for him to arrive, must have been like standing in the Oval Office awaiting the president—very intimidating. But there they stood, shuffling their clean feet, wondering if he would be angry and what their fate might be. Then Joseph entered the room.

Read Genesis 43:26–29.

Immediately, the brothers offered their gifts and bowed to the ground. Joseph spoke to them, not out of anger, but out of concern. How was their aged father? Was he still alive? (Genesis 43:27).

Looking into each face—knowing each by name—Joseph focused on the youngest, Benjamin. His face was no longer that of a child, smooth and pudgy, but that of a young man, tanned and rugged. Joseph knew Benjamin in an instant, but in order to hide his identity, he asked if this young man was the one they had spoken of earlier. Then he blessed Benjamin: "May God be gracious to you, my son" (43:29).

 Read Genesis 43:30–31.

Twenty years of longing and love, of regret and sadness, had been held at bay by a great dam within Joseph's heart. But the sight of Benjamin caused a fissure that burst forth in a flood of emotion.

Joseph ran to his bedroom and wept (Genesis 43:30). Then, composing himself, he dried his tears, washed his face, and came back into the room. The brothers were about to receive another gift of grace from their disguised brother—a meal fit for a king (43:31).

 Read Genesis 43:32–34.

Three separate tables were set up for the meal. Joseph, as an Egyptian and prime minister, sat at the head table. The brothers sat at another table. And the Egyptian household sat at a third (Genesis 43:32).

DOORWAY TO HISTORY
Egyptian Dining Customs

Egyptians kept strict dietary customs. The Greek historian Herodotus noted that cows were sacred to Egyptians—their goddess Isis had the body of a woman and the horns of a cow—and therefore cows were not eaten. Nor would an Egyptian kiss a Greek or use a Greek's cooking utensils, because Greeks had no such prohibition against eating beef.[3]

Egyptian dietary customs also applied to sheep. They detested shepherds (Genesis 46:34) and would not eat the flesh of sheep—a staple in the Hebrew diet (Deuteronomy 14:4). Egyptians viewed themselves as racially and religiously superior to their foreign neighbors; clean as opposed to unclean.[4] Therefore, they "could not eat bread with the Hebrews, for that is loathsome to the Egyptians" (Genesis 43:32). It's no surprise then that Joseph and his Hebrew brothers were seated at separate tables.

The brothers surely noticed that someone had arranged their seating in order, from the oldest to the youngest—Reuben to Benjamin (43:33). They were flabbergasted. How could this be? What did the man know about them?

And if this weren't enough, Joseph served them food from his own table, in violation of Egyptian custom, and gave Benjamin five servings of everything. Imagine—five rolls, five helpings of mashed potatoes and peas, five ears of corn on the cob, five pieces of fried chicken, five glasses of iced tea. They must have rolled Benjamin out of the house. Why was such grace lavished on Benjamin? He was Joseph's full brother. And Joseph may have been testing the others. Would they resent the special treatment lavished on the youngest? Not this time. They were no longer fearful but grateful, feasting and drinking freely with their unrecognized brother (43:34).

When they have offended you, how difficult is it for you to *give* grace (blessing, acceptance, favor, or forgiveness—with no strings attached) to the following?

	Easy				Difficult
Stranger	1	2	3	4	5
Friend	1	2	3	4	5
Parents	1	2	3	4	5
In-laws	1	2	3	4	5
Siblings	1	2	3	4	5
Children	1	2	3	4	5
Spouse	1	2	3	4	5

Plot your results on the graph below, drawing a line to connect the dots.

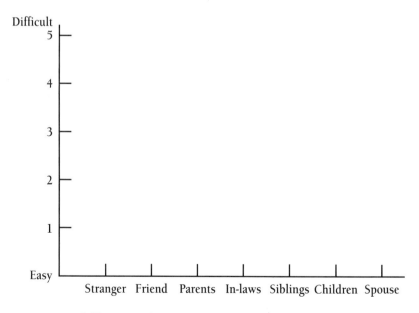

Now, using a different color pen or a pencil, add your results from the question on page 82 to the graph.

Were your results the same for both giving grace and receiving grace? If not, why do you think they're different? Is it easier for you to give grace or receive grace? Does the identity of the giver or recipient matter to you?

_____

_____

_____

_____

STARTING YOUR JOURNEY

Joseph's life offers us a magnificent portrayal of the grace of God as He came to our rescue in the person of His Son, Jesus Christ. We come to God as Joseph's guilty brothers came to Joseph, feeling the distance and fearing the worst, only to have God demonstrate incredible generosity and mercy. Instead of being blamed, we are forgiven. Instead of being imprisoned by guilt, we are freed. And instead of experiencing punishment, which we certainly deserve, we are seated at His table and served more than we can ever take in.

Some of us may accept the gift of grace but have trouble acknowledging it in our daily lives. We may withdraw from God, allowing ourselves to wallow in guilt and shame. Or we may desperately plead our guilty case before Him, fearing punishment and condemnation. Other times, we try bargaining with Him with good deeds, thinking our hard work and sincere efforts will pay Him back for our evil actions. What we have in mind is to earn just enough forgiveness to silence our guilt, but what He has in mind is to overwhelm us with such an abundance that we realize we can never, ever repay Him.

Consider the beautiful picture of Christ at the cross, bearing the sins we committed, forgiving us in the process. Isn't it amazing? The One who was rejected is the same One who invites us to a banquet, serving the things we hunger for. The table is loaded, and He is smiling, waiting for us to sit down and enjoy the feast.

God's demonstration of grace to us will never be matched. Using the letters G-R-A-C-E, what word(s) can you think of to describe the nature of His grace?

G_____

R_____

A_____

C_____

E_____

Have you chosen to accept the gift of God's grace (salvation)? Or are you still wrestling with fear and guilt? Write your thoughts below.

_____

_____

_____

If you have accepted God's gift, do you believe He has forgiven you fully, no strings attached? Do you live in that abundance daily, keeping short accounts with God, or do you live in fear and guilt, bargaining with God or pleading with Him when you fall?

_____

_____

_____

What light does the story of Joseph and his brothers shed on your situation?

_____

_____

_____

Author Philip Yancey wrote, "I've found that words tend to spoil over the years, like old meat. Their meaning rots away. . . . *Grace* . . . is one grand theological word that has not spoiled. . . . Every English usage I can find retains some glory of the original."[5] Grace is always available; it is steadfast. Grace reminds us that there is forgiveness and assurance in the midst of blame and doubt. Are you famished from years of guilt and fear? Then have a seat—grace is being served.

"I AM JOSEPH!"

Genesis 44:1–45:15

THE HEART OF THE MATTER

"The final proof of greatness lies in being able to endure contumely [contemptuous treatment] without resentment."[1] Joseph is undoubtedly one of the greatest men of the Bible. Yet he never did any of the things we usually associate with biblical greatness, like performing miracles, slaying giants, or defeating pagan prophets. Nor did he ever write a single word of Scripture. He was just a plain, ordinary man who grew up in a dysfunctional family. So what made Joseph so great? Why does the Lord devote so much space in Genesis to tell his story? It's simple, really. Joseph was set apart by his *attitude*. He was great, not because of some miraculous action, but because he demonstrated a daily positive attitude toward God and toward others. And his example stands as a challenge for us today.

DISCOVERING THE WAY

If a positive attitude is the test of greatness, then Joseph aced the exam. But his attitude was not the "power of positive thinking" variety. Rather, he possessed a God-focused perspective.

In your own words, what makes a person truly great?

_____

_____

_____

Look at your answer above. Circle each attitude-oriented word, and put a square around each action-oriented word. Now, count the number of words in each group, and place the totals below.

Attitude	Action

What do the numbers reveal regarding your perception of greatness?

_____

_____

_____

The story of Joseph and his encounter with his brothers reveals that greatness in God's eyes is composed of a positive attitude that looks up and out.

THE TRAP: SILVER IN THE SACK

In contrast to Joseph, his brothers were selfish and callous. Joseph remembered that all too well. Desiring to see if they had developed a positive mind-set toward God and a positive response to others, Joseph devised a little test using an expensive silver cup.

 Read Genesis 44:1–5.

As soon as the feast ended, Joseph took his butler aside and told him to place the brothers' money in their sacks and fill them with grain, just as he had done upon their previous departure (Genesis 42:25). Joseph then instructed him to place one other item in Benjamin's sack—Joseph's silver cup (44:1–2).

The next morning, the brothers expressed their gratitude to Joseph for his hospitality and happily left for Canaan. The little caravan of eleven brothers and their donkeys had barely crossed the city limits when Joseph ordered his butler to apprehend them and accuse them of stealing his silver cup (44:3–5).

 Read Genesis 44:6–13.

Catching up with the eleven, the butler did as he was told, accusing the brothers of repaying "evil for good" (Genesis 44:4). In a desperate panic, they vehemently denied the charge. They tried to defend themselves. What reason could they possibly have to steal from the prime minister (44:6–8)?

They should have stopped there, but they didn't. Just as talkative and defensive as before (43:20–22), the brothers offered their lives on a silver platter, confident that they would be vindicated. The butler agreed that the life of the thief would be forfeited, but rather than facing death as the brothers had promised, he would become the prime minister's slave, and the others would be allowed to return home.

When the cup was found in Benjamin's sack (44:9–12), the brothers were horrified. Ripping their clothes as a sign of great grief, they did something extraordinary—they returned to Egypt to face punishment with Benjamin. They didn't abandon their little brother this time (44:13).

 Read Genesis 44:14–17.

Upon returning to Joseph's house, the brothers threw themselves at his feet (Genesis 44:14). The trap had been sprung. The brothers were caught in the jaws of unfair circumstances, just as Joseph had once been. And like flies on flypaper, they were unable to escape.

But Judah decided to try. Looking up into the stern face of the prime minister, he pled guilty: "God has found out the iniquity of your servants" (44:16). Finally, a confession came from a broken and contrite heart. But this was not an admission of guilt regarding the cup. This confession was twenty years in the making. And with it, Judah and his brothers passed Joseph's first test: sensitivity to God's work in their lives.

Read Genesis 44:16. What evidence do you find that Judah's perspective had changed?

_____

_____

_____

Joseph then dismissed the brothers, but he declared that Benjamin would have to remain in Egypt as his slave (Genesis 44:17).

THE BARGAIN: BROTHER FOR THE BROTHER

After Judah's great confession, why didn't Joseph reveal himself? Why continue the ruse and threaten to enslave Benjamin? Joseph was devising another test for his brothers. By placing Benjamin in a similar situation to the one Joseph was in twenty years earlier, Joseph targeted their hearts. The brothers passed the vertical, godly test, but would they pass the horizontal, human one? Were they sensitive to the needs of others? Would they stand with Benjamin regardless of the cost? And what of Jacob—would they tell him another lie about a lost son?

 Read Genesis 44:18–29.

Judah, who twenty years earlier had hatched the idea of selling Joseph (Genesis 37:26–27), delivered a magnificent speech begging for the lives of Benjamin and Jacob. He opened with a conciliatory note: "my lord . . . do not be angry . . . you are equal to Pharaoh" (44:18). This was not mere flattery. Joseph _was_ equal to Pharaoh; he held Benjamin's life in his hands.

Judah reminded the prime minister of their first visit to Egypt and the events that had since taken place (44:19–23). Interestingly, he highlighted Jacob's fear of losing Benjamin just as he had lost Joseph twenty years before (44:27–29). Back then Judah had been too proud to care. He cared now. Spiritually, he had grown up.

Read Genesis 44:30–34.

The consequences of leaving Benjamin in Egypt were dire—the life or death of Jacob (Genesis 44:30–31). So Judah offered a compromise: his life for Benjamin's (44:32–33).

Then Judah concluded his speech with a question that ultimately broke the prime minister's coldhearted veneer. "How shall I go up to my father . . . for fear that I see the evil that would overtake [him]" (44:34)?

How would you characterize Judah's attitude in this passage?

_____

_____

_____

How did Judah model the characteristics of a godly attitude found in the following verses?

Philippians 2:3–8

_____

_____

_____

James 4:10

_____

_____

_____

1 John 3:16, 20

_____

_____

_____

THE DISCLOSURE: IDENTITY OF THE GOVERNOR

These were clearly not the same brothers who sold Joseph into slavery twenty years earlier. Like the Grinch in Dr. Seuss's classic tale *How the Grinch Stole Christmas!* their hearts had grown three sizes. They were mature enough to see God's sovereign hand in their lives and selfless enough to sacrifice their own lives for their little brother. It was too much for Joseph—he could wear the mask no longer. They now modeled the characteristics Joseph himself had learned.

 Read Genesis 45:1–4.

Joseph ordered his servants out of the room (Genesis 45:1). Then he broke down and wailed (45:2). Fighting back the tears, Joseph cried out in Hebrew, saying words they never thought they would hear: *Aaa-Nee Yo-saphe*—"I am Joseph!" And then, "Is my father still alive?" The brothers were dumbfounded. In fact, they were absolutely terrified (45:3).

Seeing the shock on his brothers' faces, he told them to "come closer." He said to them, "I am your brother Joseph, whom you sold into Egypt" (45:4).

THE RESPONSE: GRACE TO THE GUILTY

The greatness of Joseph came into full bloom as he revealed a sensitivity toward God and deep compassion toward his brothers.

 Read Genesis 45:5–8.

A lesser man would have punished the brothers for what they had done. But not Joseph. He knew his brothers were overwhelmed with anxiety and guilt. His first reaction was compassion and support: "Do not be grieved or angry" (Genesis 45:5).

How could Joseph demonstrate such kindness? He had maintained a godward perspective in the trials of his life. Three times Joseph told his brothers that God was the one who had sent him to Egypt, to save lives from the sickle of famine (45:5–8). The brothers may have been the means, but it was God who had arranged for Joseph to become prime minister of Egypt (45:8).

In addition to having a vertical perspective, Joseph ranked high in compassion toward others, generosity, and forgiveness. How would you rank yourself in these areas?

Unfeeling				Compassionate
1	2	3	4	5

Stingy				Generous
1	2	3	4	5

Unforgiving				Forgiving
1	2	3	4	5

What attitudes do the following verses command us to demonstrate?

Ephesians 4:32

_____

_____

_____

Colossians 3:12–13

_____

_____

_____

1 Timothy 6:18

_____

_____

_____

With which attitude do you tend to struggle the most?

_____

_____

_____

 Read Genesis 45:9–13.

With excitement and impatience, Joseph commanded his brothers to hurry back to Canaan to tell Jacob what God had done in his life. He told them to ask Jacob to pack up the family and move (Genesis 45:9).

Joseph planned to settle the family in the garden spot of Egypt—Goshen. There had been too much distance between them for too long. No more. The whole family was to live close to Joseph, his brothers included. Five years of famine remained, and Joseph longed to provide for his father and his family (45:10–13).

 Read Genesis 45:14–15.

The grace of compassion and generosity is made complete by total forgiveness. Falling upon Benjamin's neck, Joseph wept. And then going to each brother, he kissed them. At long last, Joseph was reconciled with his brothers (Genesis 45:14–15).

STARTING YOUR JOURNEY

We've seen that Joseph's greatness was revealed not in some miraculous action but in his daily positive attitude toward God and others. How can we tell if we have the right attitude?

First, *when we're able to see God's plan in our location, we're getting the right attitude.* Remember what Joseph said to his brothers: "God sent me. . . . God sent me. . . . It was not you who sent me here, but God" (Genesis 45:5, 7–8).

Where do you live and work right now?

_____

What is your attitude toward your location? Are you happy? Unhappy? Why?

_____

_____

_____

Can you see God's plan in your location? If so, write a prayer of thanks below. If not, pray that God would open your eyes to see His sovereignty in placing you where you are.

_____

_____

_____

If necessary, what do you need to change so you can be faithful where you are?

_____

_____

_____

Second, *when we're able to sense God's hand in our situation, we're getting the right attitude.* Joseph told his brothers that God had made him prime minister of Egypt (45:8–9). He gave God the credit for bringing him into this position of authority. He saw God's purpose in it all—even his slavery and imprisonment.

Do you actively look for God's hand moving in your life? What clues might tip you off to His involvement?

_____

_____

_____

Do you give God credit for the good things? What about the bad things? Do you tend to blame Him? If so, why do you think you feel this way?

_____

_____

_____

Third, *when we're able to accept both as good, even when there's been evil in the process, we're getting the right attitude.* When we can be faithful in our location and trust Him in our situation, even if it is difficult, then we are looking at life with a godly perspective. It is then that we begin to model the godly attitude displayed by Joseph and eventually by his brothers.

Read Romans 8:28. How should this truth impact your daily attitude?

_____

_____

_____

Many of us strive to achieve greatness through some great accomplishment, sacrificing everything in the pursuit. But in doing so, we starve our character and our souls, and true greatness eludes us. Greatness is not found in something we *do*; it's found in something we *are*—our attitude. Joseph wasn't born with a godly attitude; it was something he had to cultivate. We must do the same. A good place to start is by maintaining a godward focus—watching for God's sovereign hand at work in our everyday lives—and by treating others with respect and kindness.

THE ULTIMATE FAMILY REUNION

Genesis 45:16–46:30

THE HEART OF THE MATTER

Few things are more poignant than the reconciliation and reunion of a family long separated by distance or circumstance. The story of Joseph provides a moving example not just of reconciliation but of long-awaited reunion. Studying the reunion of Joseph and Jacob reminds us of that joyful day when we will be united with our heavenly Father. As we wait for the reunion of the family of God, how do we prepare? We live today in light of eternity.

DISCOVERING THE WAY

Joseph anticipated being reunited with his father within a couple of weeks of sending his brothers to get him, depending on how long it took them to travel back to Canaan and bring their father to Egypt.

PLANS FOR THE REUNION

Joseph told his brothers he would relocate them to Egypt, giving them the very best land for their home (Genesis 45:10), but he hadn't consulted with Pharaoh. What would Pharaoh think about Joseph giving his family prime real estate?

 Read Genesis 45:16–20.

People love to wag their tongues about others, especially about those in positions of power. Once the ancient rumor mill ground its way to the throne room, Pharaoh quickly dispatched a message approving Joseph's plan to move the family. But Pharaoh didn't want to relocate them just anywhere. He offered them the "best of the land of Egypt" (Genesis 45:16–18), just as Joseph had promised.

Going one step further, Pharaoh provided wagons to expedite the move from Canaan to Egypt. Joseph's family was not to worry about their goods—they were to leave them all behind—because the very best of Egypt awaited them (45:19–20). What a glorious gift!

List your most prized material possessions.

1. _____

2. _____

3. _____

4. _____

5. _____

Do you think it will be difficult to leave these things behind someday? Why, or why not?

_____

_____

_____

How do heaven's riches compare to your most prized posses-sions? Does Revelation 21:10, 18–22 affect your perspective?

_____

_____

_____

Read Genesis 45:21–24.

Joseph immediately did as he had been commanded by Pharaoh. He rounded up wagons, opened up the storehouses, and ordered supplies. For Jacob, Joseph loaded down ten male donkeys with the finest Egyptian clothes, goods, and delicacies and ten female donkeys with enough food to feed him like an Egyptian prince (Genesis 45:23). It must have been an unbelievable sight—a caravan of such overwhelming abundance, passing through a famine-scarred land strewn with the carcasses of dead animals.

Each brother received a new tunic with a matching belt and sandals. And Benjamin received five times more than his brothers (45:21–22)! All this newfound wealth—especially that given to Benjamin—had the potential of raising old jealousies, so Joseph instructed his brothers: "Do not quarrel" (45:24). The Hebrew word is *ragaz*, meaning to "be agitated . . . perturbed," and it is often used preceding a fight.[1] His brothers may have confessed and been reconciled to him, but they were still human! Joseph was concerned they might still be quarrelsome and combative. He wanted them to live in the knowledge of the grace they had received and the great things that awaited them in Egypt.

Similarly, living today with eternity in mind means adjusting our attitudes. According to James 4:1–2, what usually causes arguments and conflicts?

_____

_____

_____

What should we do with our argumentative and malicious tendencies? (See Colossians 3:8 and 1 Peter 2:1 for help. For more insight, try looking up these verses in several different Bible versions.)

_____

_____

_____

What should we put in their place, according to Philippians 4:8 and Colossians 3:1–2?

_____

_____

_____

God has given believers in Christ the assurance that we will be with Him in heaven for eternity. Why do you think He cares so much about our daily actions on earth?

_____

_____

_____

_____

_____

 Read Genesis 45:25–28.

Apparently, while on their journey, the brothers didn't argue about the pettiness of possessions. They were probably thinking about how to tell Jacob that Joseph was alive and well in Egypt. Questions would inevitably come: "What about the blood-stained coat?" "How did Joseph end up in Egypt?" "Did you lie to me?" They decided that blunt honesty was the best option.

Dressed to the hilt in their designer tunics, they walked up to Jacob, who had been watching this caravan approaching, and came right out with the news: "Joseph is still alive, and indeed he is ruler over all the land of Egypt" (Genesis 45:26). No confession of their sin. No long explanation. No softened greeting. "Joseph is alive, and he's the prime minister of Egypt." Just simple and direct.

How did Jacob take the news? The Hebrew words in Genesis 45:26 are translated literally as "his heart grew numb."[2] Most likely, Jacob had a mild heart attack. Seeing their father's reaction, the brothers sat him down and explained what Joseph had said to them. Hearing these words and seeing the wagons and donkeys loaded with goods, Jacob's spirit was revived (45:27). And he responded as any loving father would: "I will go and see him before I die" (45:28).

Journey from Canaan to Egypt

No doubt the brothers told Jacob about Joseph's desire to relocate the family to Egypt. But pulling up tent stakes and moving to a foreign land filled with foreign gods and customs is a life-altering decision. Impetuous by nature, Jacob had finally learned to seek the Lord before rushing ahead.

 Read Genesis 46:1–4.

Relocating to Egypt was not simply a personal move for Jacob and his family. It was a national move, affecting the entire nation of Israel. This is indicated by the Bible's use of Jacob's national name, "Israel" (Genesis 46:1).

Making his way south to Beersheba, Jacob sought the Lord, offering sacrifices (46:1). His little nation was about to cross over into a fast-paced, polytheistic society that could swallow them whole. He needed to know, should he make such a move?

Moving, changing careers, starting a family—each is a life-altering event. What is your usual process for making major decisions?

_____

_____

_____

How does knowing of the certainty of God's presence with you now and of your future reunion with the Lord affect your decision-making in situations like these?

_____

_____

_____

Read Philippians 4:6–7 and fill in the key words below, keeping in mind that an eternal perspective is not only pleasing to God but also offers a present promise.

"Be _____ for nothing, but in _____ by _____ and _____ with _____ let your _____ be made known to _____. And the _____ of God, which _____ all _____, will _____ your _____ and your _____ in Christ Jesus."

After seeking God and hearing from Him, the next morning Jacob woke with confidence. The Lord had told him not to be afraid, because He would make him into a great nation (Genesis 46:2–3). God promised Jacob that He would accompany him on his journey. Jacob also learned that he would die in Egypt. God didn't tell him how long his descendants would live there or how large the nation of Israel would grow, but He did promise that one day the nation would return to Canaan, effectively foreshadowing the Exodus (46:4).

 Read Genesis 46:5–7 and 26–27.

LESSON TEN   *The Ultimate Family Reunion*

With the blessing of God, Jacob and his entire family—the seedling of the nation of Israel—loaded the wagons and headed south. They placed Jacob, the women, and the children in the wagons, while the men walked. Though Pharaoh promised to provide for their every need (Genesis 45:20), the family did bring along their possessions, soon arriving in the land of Egypt to start a new life. From a small seed—seventy of Jacob's male descendants and their families—the Lord would grow a nation (Israel) within a nation (Egypt).

Jacob and his family relocated with hope in their hearts, having faith in their promised reunion. Like Jacob, we too obey though we don't know exactly what to expect, trusting God's promise of His presence with us now and at the end of our life's journey.

What does God promise us we can anticipate about our heavenly reunion with Him?

John 14:2–3

_____

Philippians 3:20–21

_____

Revelation 7:16–17

_____

Revelation 21:3–4

_____

REUNION WITH JOSEPH

When the tiny nation of Israel crossed the border, they must have looked ragged. These dirty, smelly Hebrews, with their musty sheep, must have appeared as the dregs of the earth as they plodded past the sophisticated and well-appointed Egyptians. They weren't even sure where to go!

Read Genesis 46:28–30.

Jacob sent Judah ahead to ask Joseph for directions. Finding their way, the little nation of Israel began to unpack and set up camp in the fertile valley of Goshen (Genesis 46:28).

Joseph had been waiting for this day for twenty years. He washed his chariot and struck out for Goshen. Imagine—he probably broke every speed limit there was, pushing his horses faster and faster. Then, jumping off his chariot—maybe even before it came to a complete stop—Joseph ran to his father and embraced him with tears of utter delight.

Linger here for a moment. Imagine the scene. No words were spoken. What could be said? Father and son were reunited, embracing each other with tears of joy. Neither letting the other go. Hugging so tight it was as if they would enter each other's skin. And they did this for a "long time" (46:29).

Pulling away for just a moment, cupping Joseph's face in his hands, Jacob, through a cloud of tears, declared his life complete. "Now let me die, since I have seen your face, that you are still alive" (46:30).

 STARTING YOUR JOURNEY

Family reunions are wonderful events, especially when distance has been caused by disappointment or sin. The Bible speaks of other joy-filled reunions, like the *national reunion* found in Ezra 8 or the *personal reunion* of another father who lost a son in Luke 15:11–32.

Each of these are wonderful and moving stories, but the greatest reunion is yet to come. It is the one all children of God long for—being reunited with our heavenly Father. And best of all, the *ultimate family reunion* is an eternal reunion.

Read 1 Thessalonians 4:13–18. Summarize this passage in your own words. What great future event is this passage describing?

_____

_____

_____

Knowing that "the rapture" awaits Christians in the future, how does 1 Thessalonians 2:10–12 command us to live?

_____

_____

_____

As you consider your reunion with the Holy One who loves you and created you, are there areas of your life that you would be ashamed for Him to see, areas that don't reflect your future citizenship in heaven? With complete honesty, rank how worthy or pleasing your walk is in each area of your life.

	Worthy				Unworthy
Attitudes	1	2	3	4	5
Finances	1	2	3	4	5
Marriage	1	2	3	4	5
Children	1	2	3	4	5
Purity	1	2	3	4	5

How do you feel when you consider your answers to the previous question? Joyful? Convicted? Are there areas that need to change in order for your life to reflect the future that lies ahead of you? If so, what are they?

_____

_____

_____

Thinking practically, what can you do this week to begin to address these areas? Be specific.

_____

_____

_____

⁂

Many live their lives under the notion that life is about the here-and-now, but it isn't. Life is actually leading up to eternity. Solomon wrote that God has "set eternity in [our] heart[s]" (Ecclesiastes 3:11). We are made for the ever after, to live either with Christ or apart from Him. But we are currently trapped in time. The challenge for us, then, is to live today in light of eternity. Preparing our hearts and living with an eternal mind-set in the present will make our heavenly reunion all the sweeter. And oh, what a day that will be!

ON-THE-JOB INTEGRITY
Genesis 46:31–47:26

THE HEART OF THE MATTER

Can you be a person of integrity and a successful businessperson at the same time? More than a century ago, the great preacher Phillips Brooks admonished Christian professionals from the pulpit of Trinity Church on Wall Street "to show how [they] . . . shall purify and lift the business that [they do] and make it the worthy occupation of the Son of God."[1] In a word, Brooks was talking about the timeless quality of *integrity*. Christians are to demonstrate how God would negotiate a deal, try a case, diagnose an illness, teach a class, or build a building. Joseph is a perfect example—he demonstrated integrity in every aspect of his life. And by observing his business life, we'll learn how to order our priorities and test our motives.

DISCOVERING THE WAY

Brooks eloquently stated that "there rests an awful and a beautiful responsibility" for Christians "to prove . . . that [business is] capable of being made divine . . . that a man can do the work . . . and yet shall love his God and his fellow-man as himself."[2] If there ever was such a man who balanced his business life with a deep, active love for God and others, it was Joseph.

SOME GENERAL OBSERVATIONS ABOUT BUSINESS

Before we turn the page on Joseph's business ledger, let's take a moment to consider how business can affect our Christian witness.

First, *work reveals our character*. Sadly, too many Christians are Sunday-morning Christians and Monday-morning heathens. They are incapable of making their work divine. How can you tell? Observe their character over a forty-hour workweek. Do they demonstrate positive traits or negative traits? How do they approach their work? How do they treat other people?

Make a list of negative and positive character traits that people commonly display on the job, such as laziness, dishonesty, loyalty, or diligence.

Negative	Positive

Circle at least one trait in each box that applies to your own work life. Then come up with a few ways to improve the negative(s) and build on the positive(s).

_____

_____

_____

Second, *work is a demanding arena of pressure*. Some jobs test the limits of a Christian's love for God and others. Every job brings pressure—office politics, deadlines, criticism, evaluations, pettiness. . . . The list could go on and on. The pressure-cooker of business causes true beliefs to bubble to the surface.

Read the following terms, then write down the first word that comes to mind in response to each one.

Deadline _____   Meetings _____

Evaluation _____   Supervisor _____

Vacation _____   Monday _____

Layoffs _____   To-Do List _____

Paycheck _____   Colleagues _____

Did your responses tend to evoke negative or positive emotions? What might they reveal about the amount of pressure you're feeling at work?

_____

_____

_____

Briefly describe how you currently handle pressure at work. Then describe one or two strategies you might use to relieve some of the pressure you're experiencing.

_____

_____

_____

_____

Third, *work is an exacting test of efficiency.* All jobs require some level of efficiency; some standards must be met. But if you are an inefficient worker, your tasks can be a chore rather than a joy.

To find out if you tend to be efficient or inefficient, take this short test. Rank yourself according to each category.

Disorganized				Organized
1	2	3	4	5

Indecisive				Decisive
1	2	3	4	5

Unmotivated				Self-Motivated
1	2	3	4	5

Uncreative				Creative
1	2	3	4	5

Reactive				Proactive
1	2	3	4	5

Add your total, and place the result here: _____

Divide that number by 5, and place the result here: _____

Note where you fall on the following scale.

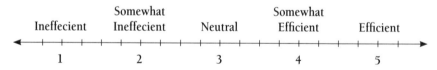

	Somewhat		Somewhat	
Ineffecient	Ineffecient	Neutral	Efficient	Efficient
1	2	3	4	5

Can you pinpoint specific areas in which you need to address a lack of efficiency? What are they? What do you need to do to become more efficient?

_____

_____

_____

A SPECIFIC EXAMPLE: JOSEPH

If Joseph had written a book on business efficiency and integrity or on crisis management and leadership, his table of contents would have included at least four traits every professional should possess. Joseph modeled them for us.

 Read Genesis 46:31–34.

With his family now relocated in Egypt, Joseph didn't abuse his position as prime minister and presume upon Pharaoh by permanently settling his family in Goshen. He didn't remind Pharaoh that he was the one who had warned Egypt about the famine so Pharaoh would offer special privileges to his family. No, Joseph didn't do any of these things. Rather, *he planned ahead with wise objectivity.*

Joseph knew the Egyptian mind-set. He was wise enough to understand that he shouldn't just march a ragtag group of shepherds into the throne room of a king. So, in order to get his family settled well, Joseph carefully prepared the way for the introduction of his family (Genesis 46:31–32). He instructed his brothers in what they should and shouldn't say when they appeared before Pharaoh. He encouraged them to say that they were "keepers of livestock" rather than shepherds, because "every shepherd is loathsome to the Egyptians" (46:33–34).

Joseph's advice to his brothers makes shrewd business and cultural sense, but does it dance over the line of honesty? Why, or why not?

_____

_____

_____

In Matthew 10:16, Jesus instructs His disciples to be "shrewd as serpents and innocent as doves" as they minister in a harsh, sinful world. As a Christian professional, how can you be shrewd, yet maintain your integrity?

_____

_____

_____

 Read Genesis 47:1–6.

Joseph was a powerful man, but he was a man under authority. He didn't want to do anything that might appear as usurpation or give Pharaoh any indication that he wasn't completely faithful. So, _he submitted to authority with loyal accountability._

Just as he had planned, Joseph went to Pharaoh and told him that his family had arrived from Canaan and were camping in Goshen (Genesis 47:1). He introduced Pharaoh to five of his brothers (47:2).

Then came the question that could have caused Joseph to shake in his sandals — Pharaoh asked the brothers what they did for a living. "Your servants are shepherds," they replied (47:3).

They didn't follow the script, but Joseph was a flexible leader. He let them tell their story in their own words. Joseph didn't have to worry; he had already demonstrated his loyalty to Pharaoh, and he would continue to do so.

Upon meeting Joseph's brothers, Pharaoh threw open the doors of Egypt. Joseph's family was welcome to live in Goshen. And if any of them were especially skilled, Pharaoh asked them to tend his flocks as well (47:5–6). Pharaoh trusted Joseph so much, he automatically extended trust to the other members of Joseph's family, expecting to find the same skill and sound judgment he found in Joseph.

 Read Genesis 47:7–12.

Whew! Once the question of location was answered, Joseph brought his beloved father to meet Pharaoh. When Jacob saw the king of Egypt, he blessed him. Then Joseph settled his family in the land and provided food for his whole clan.

 Read Genesis 47:13–19.

As the keeper of the keys to the granaries, Joseph could have easily taken advantage of the people's desperate plight. With all the comings and goings and exchange of money for grain, who would miss a few dollars here or there? Pharaoh certainly wasn't keeping an accounting—that was Joseph's job. Or how about raising the prices and gouging the people? Joseph could have put the actual cost of the grain in the bank and pocketed the excess. After all, the laws of supply and demand were at work, weren't they?

Lesser men would have succumbed to these temptations, but Joseph had too much integrity. He turned every dime over to the treasury (Genesis 47:13–14). *He arranged for survival with personal integrity.*

Joseph's integrity developed from two main character traits, among others. Look at Genesis 41:33 and identify these two traits. Then, using a dictionary, define each one.

1. _____

_____

2. _____

_____

How can you incorporate these two traits into your own character? (See James 1:5 for guidance.)

_____

_____

_____

Desperation deepened when the money ran out (Genesis 47:15). Yet with wisdom and discernment, Joseph helped the people maintain their dignity and survive. To allow them to provide for their own families, the people could exchange their livestock for grain (47:16–17).

Within a year the people had no more livestock to sell, and yet the famine persisted. All they had left were their lands and their own bodies. Crying out to Joseph, they willingly sold themselves and their lands to Pharaoh for food (47:18–19).

 Read Genesis 47:20–26.

Joseph was never one of those who stifled new ideas with a "We've never done that before" attitude. He couldn't afford such defeatist thinking—lives were at stake. So what did Joseph do with millions of starving people? *He accepted the challenge with innovative creativity.*

The people had a plan—they would sell themselves and their lands to Pharaoh in exchange for food. Joseph took the people's idea and combined it with his own. Joseph bought the land of all the people except the priests, and to insure future productivity he redistributed the population to various cities in Egypt (Genesis 47:20–22).

The relocation of an entire population was innovative and required great creativity as well as an efficient plan and a widespread trust in Joseph's integrity. He gave them seed to sow the land and instituted a tax, ensuring the treasury's solvency and the people's salvation. One-fifth of the harvest was paid to Pharaoh, and four-fifths was allowed as income to the people (47:23–24). The plan was so successful, it won hearty approval from the people. Joseph wrote the levy into law (47:25–26).

STARTING YOUR JOURNEY

Author and speaker John Maxwell has rightly said that "People with integrity are 'whole' people; they can be identified by their single-mindedness." [3] This was certainly true of Joseph, and it should be true of all Christians, especially as it is reflected in our priorities and motives.

Our highest priority as Christian professionals should be our *commitment to Christian principles.* If we have to deceive, lie, or step on people to succeed, then we've failed. Oh, we might climb to the top rung of the corporate ladder, but in the end we'll discover that the ladder was leaning against the wrong wall.

Read the following Scriptures and identify the principles they contain for Christian businesspeople.

Ephesians 6:5–6

_____

_____

_____

Colossians 3:22–25

_____

_____

_____

2 Thessalonians 3:10

_____

_____

_____

Titus 2:9–10

_____

_____

_____

1 Peter 2:18–20

_____

_____

_____

Our other priority should be the *careful investment of time.* The great lexicographer Samuel Johnson observed, "Human moments are stolen away by a thousand petty impediments which leave no trace behind them."[4] Perhaps the hardest word to say in the English language is the easiest to spell: N–O.

Take a moment to analyze your work priorities. Are you investing your time wisely? Do you tend to invest in frivolous, unimportant, or foolish things? When you say yes to these things, what are you consequently saying no to?

_____

_____

_____

_____

_____

_____

If your priorities are out of balance, make a list of things to which you should say no.

_____

_____

_____

_____

Write out a script you can use to say no when you are asked or pressured to commit to a responsibility or attend an event that is not a wise use of your time and energy. (It should be gracious, yet firm, and include a positive reason for why you are saying no.)

_____

_____

_____

_____

_____

Our motives must be pure, *continually watching how we relate to people and asking* why *we said yes or no to each request.* As business professionals who are Christians, we must always treat people with dignity and respect, show humility, and remember for whom we ultimately work—the Lord.

Is it possible to be a person of integrity and a successful business-person? The answer is *yes.* A little strategic planning, a pinch of loyalty, a handful of honesty, and a dash of creativity are the ingredients of success. And along with right priorities and pure motives, they will produce a life of integrity, much like Joseph's.

HIGHLIGHTS OF TWILIGHT AND MIDNIGHT

Genesis 47:27–50:26

THE HEART OF THE MATTER

When your loved ones gather to reminisce about your life, what memories will they share? What do you hope they will remember? The story of Joseph's life—his journey from the pit to the pinnacle—is remarkable. Few have known such highs and lows, and fewer still have lived a life so full of grace and forgiveness. And as we have discovered in our study of this extraordinary man, if we choose to follow Joseph's example, our lives can be marked by such noble traits, creating a spiritual legacy for those who come after us. What greater memory could we leave to those who love us than that of a life well-lived—full of grace and truth?

DISCOVERING THE WAY

We've come to the end of Joseph's story. The last chapters have been written, and the book will soon be closed. But before we turn the last page, we have a lesson or two left to learn as Joseph buries his father and passes away himself. We'll learn how to live life in the "twilight" and the "midnight," the near-end and end of our days.

Most of us don't live today with the end in mind. We're too busy, or we think it best to avoid the subject of death altogether. But death is inevitable. And only memories will remain after we're gone. With that in mind, if you were to write your own eulogy, what would you like it to say?

_____

_____

_____

_____

JACOB: SICKNESS, BLESSING, AND DEATH

The joyous and tear-filled reunion between father and son led to many rich years of fellowship. And their renewed relationship continued until the dignified and sorrowful death of the patriarch, Jacob.

 Read Genesis 47:27–31.

When Jacob moved his family to Egypt, he was 130 years old and the famine was in its second year (Genesis 45:11). Seventeen years later, with the famine behind them, the tiny nation of Israel had settled permanently in Goshen and had flourished there (47:27–28).

How sweet those years must have been for Jacob—to see Joseph rule with authority and integrity, to see his family growing.

But Jacob became ill, and he knew he wouldn't recover. Thinking of the promise God made to his grandfather, Abraham (12:1–3), Jacob expressed his desire to be buried with his forefathers in Canaan. After promising to fulfill Jacob's request, Joseph was left with a precious memory of his father's humility as Jacob bowed before the Lord in worship (47:29–31).

During his life, Jacob exhibited rebellion and stubbornness more often than trust and obedience, but his last spiritual act left a lasting memory. Joseph could have etched on Jacob's tombstone, "He worshiped." What spiritual legacy would your spouse, your children, or a loved one chisel into your tombstone?

_____

_____

_____

Are you satisfied with that spiritual legacy? Why, or why not? What would you change, if anything?

_____

_____

_____

 Skim Genesis 48:1–22.

As Jacob's condition worsened, Joseph was again summoned to his bedside. This time Joseph brought his two sons, Manasseh and Ephraim. Jacob took time to remind his son about God's promise (Genesis 48:1–4). Then, he adopted Manasseh and Ephraim as his own sons, remembering the death of Rachel, his beloved wife, who had given him two sons (48:5–7).

By this time Manasseh and Ephraim had spent seventeen years with their granddad; they were probably in their twenties. After kissing and hugging his grandsons, Jacob repeated the pattern that had become natural in his family, blessing the younger Ephraim over the older Manasseh (48:13–20). Several times in the book of Genesis God used the act of blessing to choose the younger over the older—Jacob over Esau (27:1–40), Ephraim over Manasseh (48:8–20), and Joseph over Reuben (48:22).

Concluding the blessing, Jacob reminded Joseph of God's presence and promise and gave him a double portion of inheritance (48:21–22).

 DOORWAY TO HISTORY
The Blessing
"May God make you like Ephraim and Manasseh!" (Genesis 48:20). This ancient blessing from Jacob to his grandsons is still spoken in Jewish families today. But what exactly is a blessing?

The Hebrew word for "bless," *barak*, literally means "to kneel."[1] It conveys the idea of bowing in honor or of attaching value to someone. In the Old Testament, blessings communicated spiritual, physical, and prophetic truths. The blessing of Abraham (12:1–3) was a promise to make him into a great nation and to settle his descendants in a homeland. But the promise also carried with it a spiritual and prophetic element—that Abraham's descendants would be a great blessing to the "families of the earth." This was fulfilled in Jesus Christ, "the son of Abraham" (Matthew 1:1).

Leaving a legacy of blessing is something your loved ones will cherish for a lifetime. List the names of your children, grandchildren, or nephews and nieces. If you aren't married, list the names of family and close friends.

1. _____ 6. _____

2. _____ 7. _____

3. _____ 8. _____

4. _____ 9. _____

5. _____ 10. _____

On separate sheets of paper, write a simple blessing for each person on the list above. What do you appreciate about who he or she is? What do you hope he will become? What do you pray for her? Then mail your blessings, even if the recipients live in your house. To ensure completion of this project, write the date you will mail your blessings: _____.

 Skim Genesis 49:1–32.

As soon as his grandsons left, Jacob called his sons together and blessed each one, beginning with Reuben and ending with Benjamin (Genesis 49:1–28). And after the blessing, Jacob instructed his sons to bury him in the family plot—the cave purchased by his grandfather in the land of Canaan (49:29–32).

 Read Genesis 49:33–50:3.

As soon as he finished speaking with his sons, Jacob died. Scripture captures this beautifully: Jacob "was gathered to his people" (Genesis 49:33). The pain was almost more than Joseph could bear. Falling on his father, Joseph wept and kissed him (50:1).

Eventually composing himself, Joseph ordered the embalming of his father. When the word spread that Joseph's father had died, the whole nation mourned for seventy days (50:2–3).

Jacob reminded Joseph of God's faithfulness over the generations. Take a moment to consider the evidence of God in your life by drawing a "life map" of the highs and lows you've experienced thus far. Include the major events that have shaped your character over the years, as well as times of distance from and closeness to God.

```
┌──────────────────────────────────────────────────┐
│                                                    │
│                                                    │
│                                                    │
│                                                    │
│  Birth                                   Present   │
│                                                    │
│                                                    │
│                                                    │
└──────────────────────────────────────────────────┘
```

Determine to share your spiritual legacy with someone. Whom will it be? What encouragement, insights, or warnings might this person gain from hearing your story? How has God shown His faithfulness to you?

_____

_____

_____

_____

_____

_____

_____

JOSEPH: GRIEF, GRACE, AND GLORY

Joseph's narrative slows to the mournful cadence of a funeral procession. But an uplifting time of grace is still ahead.

 Skim Genesis 50:4–14.

When the time of mourning for Jacob ended, Joseph sought permission from Pharaoh to bury his father in their homeland of Canaan (Genesis 50:4–5). With a long funeral procession trailing behind, Joseph buried his father in the cave at Machpelah (50:6–13). Then the funeral party returned to Egypt (50:14).

 Read Genesis 50:15–21.

As soon as they arrived back in Egypt, the brothers began to relive a terrible memory—the sin of selling Joseph into slavery. What if Joseph chose to seek retribution now that Jacob was gone (Genesis 50:15)? They sent a message from their deceased father, begging Joseph to forgive their past transgression (50:16–17). They even went so far as to throw themselves at his feet and offer their lives in servitude (50:18).

Joseph wept over their fear and anxiety (50:17). They still didn't understand that they had been forgiven! Their relationships with Joseph had been restored years before. Didn't they trust him?

With a broken heart, Joseph uttered some of the most gracious and forgiving words in the Bible. He put his brothers' fears to rest, reminding them that he wasn't in the place of God with the authority to seek retribution for sin (50:19). Joseph acknowledged their sin, but his perspective was eternal, not temporal—God had ensured the salvation of thousands in Egypt through their foolishness (50:20). Joseph continued to extend grace, committing to care for their families (50:21).

Do you know someone who is "growing old gracefully"? What do you think accounts for his or her positive outlook on life?

_____

_____

_____

Read Genesis 50:22–26.

After he was fully reunited with his brothers, Joseph lived long enough to see his grandsons and great-grandsons (Genesis 50:22–23). Then, just as his father had, Joseph became aware that his time to die was fast approaching. Gathering his brothers all around, Joseph encouraged them to remember the promises of God—God would preserve and deliver them. Then he asked to be buried in the land of his fathers, Canaan (50:24–25). Simply and with dignity, Joseph died at the age of 110 (50:26). Marked by integrity, grace, and forgiveness, his was a life well-lived.

The Bible contains several models of men and women who left positive legacies. Read these brief biographies, and list a few admirable traits for each one.

Caleb (Joshua 14:6–12)

_____

_____

_____

Elizabeth (Luke 1:39–45)

_____

_____

_____

Paul (2 Timothy 4:6–8)

_____

_____

_____

STARTING YOUR JOURNEY
The last page of Joseph's life has been turned and the book
closed. But the lessons learned from his life are still being
written, even today. So before you put the book on the
shelf and get busy with your life, remember two enduring truths.

First, *to grow old free of bitterness is one of the finest legacies we can
leave behind.* A wise man once said, "It takes a long time to grow
old and cranky, so don't start now!" Unfortunately, too many people
become hardened and embittered by life instead of allowing hardships
to render them soft and humble. But we can choose our response to
difficult times and circumstances. Joseph is an excellent example of
one who left a legacy of grace and forgiveness rather than of bitter
revenge.

**Read Acts 8:22–23, Ephesians 4:30–32, and Hebrews 12:14–15.
Why do you think it is so important to God that we avoid bitterness at all costs?**

_____

_____

_____

**With the idea of leaving a legacy behind, list the top three atti-
tudes you want to exhibit in your life.**

1._____

2._____

3._____

Specifically, what do you need to do to ensure that these attitudes form the foundation of the legacy you leave behind?

_____

_____

_____

_____

The second enduring truth we can take from Joseph's life is that *to face death right with God and man is the finest way we can enter eternity.* Forgiveness is perhaps the greatest gift one can give and receive. And there is no more enduring legacy than living the words, "I forgive you."

What does Matthew 5:23–24 command us to do?

_____

_____

_____

Is there someone from whom you need to seek forgiveness? Who is that person(s)? What happened? Is anything keeping you from seeking forgiveness?

_____

_____

_____

_____

If you were to die tomorrow, would everyone in your life have assurance that you hold no grudges, that he or she is completely forgiven? Is there someone you need to forgive? Who is that person(s)? What happened? What is keeping you from forgiving this person?

_____

_____

_____

_____

What must you do either to seek forgiveness or to forgive? List a few simple steps here. When do you plan to begin?

_____

_____

_____

If you haven't received the forgiveness of God, it is waiting for you through faith in His Son, Jesus Christ. To learn how you can receive the free gift of forgiveness and eternal life, please read "How to Begin a Relationship with God" at the end of this Bible Companion.

Memories are the movies that play through the minds of those left behind, chronicling either a noble life or an ignoble one. What we do today—right now—determines the legacy we leave them. So, how do you want to be remembered? What legacy do you hope to leave as you enter your twilight and midnight years? Joseph's legacy is a good place to start—it is one of grace and forgiveness.

How to Begin a Relationship with God

The remarkable story of Joseph's life may leave many of us thinking that he was an imaginary super-Christian, not a man of flesh and bone with real struggles. But his ability to resist the allure of sexual temptation, to hold up under crushing disappointment, to maintain his integrity in his meteoric rise, and to forgive his brothers was not the result of a superhuman feat of strength. Joseph's character was shaped by his relationship with God.

Joseph's life exhibits the blessings that come from knowing God personally. Let's take some time to consider what the rest of the Bible says about this vital relationship and how we can know Him personally too. The Bible marks the path to God with four essential truths. Let's look at each marker in detail.

Our Spiritual Condition: Totally Depraved

The first truth is rather personal. One look in the mirror of Scripture, and our human condition becomes painfully clear:

> There is none righteous, not even one;
> There is none who understands,
> There is none who seeks for God;
> All have turned aside, together they have become
> useless;
> There is none who does good,
> There is not even one. (Romans 3:10–12)

We are all sinners through and through—totally depraved. Now, that doesn't mean we've committed every atrocity known to humankind. We're not as *bad* as we can be, just as *bad off* as we can be. Sin colors all our thoughts, motives, words, and actions.

You still don't believe it? Look around. Everything around us bears the smudge marks of our sinful nature. Despite our best efforts to create a perfect world, crime statistics continue to soar, divorce rates keep climbing, and families keep crumbling.

Something has gone terribly wrong in our society and in ourselves — something deadly. Contrary to how the world would repackage it, "me-first" living doesn't equal rugged individuality and freedom; it equals death. As Paul said in his letter to the Romans, "The wages of sin is death" (Romans 6:23) — our spiritual and physical death that comes from God's righteous judgment of our sin, along with all of the emotional and practical effects of this separation that we experience on a daily basis. This brings us to the second marker: God's character.

God's Character: Infinitely Holy

How can a good and just God judge us for a sinful state into which we were born? Our total depravity is only half the answer. The other half is God's infinite holiness.

The fact that we know things are not as they should be points us to a standard of goodness beyond ourselves. Our sense of injustice in life on this side of eternity implies a perfect standard of justice beyond our reality. That standard and source is God Himself. And God's standard of holiness contrasts starkly with our sinful condition.

Scripture says that "God is Light, and in Him there is no darkness at all" (1 John 1:5). He is absolutely holy, which creates a problem for us. If He is so pure, how can we who are so impure relate to Him?

Perhaps we could try being better people, try to tilt the balance in favor of our good deeds, or seek out methods for self-improvement. Throughout history, people have attempted to live up to God's standard by keeping the Ten Commandments or living by their own code of ethics. Unfortunately, no one can come close to satisfying the demands of God's law. Romans 3:20 says, "For no one can ever be made right with God by doing what the law commands. The law simply shows us how sinful we are" (NLT).

Our Need: A Substitute

So here we are, sinners by nature and sinners by choice, trying to pull ourselves up by our own bootstraps to attain a relationship with our holy Creator. But every time we try, we fall flat on our faces. We can't live a good enough life to make up for our sin, because God's standard isn't "good enough"—it's *perfection*. And we can't make amends for the offense our sin has created without dying for it.

Who can get us out of this mess?

If someone could live perfectly, honoring God's law, and would bear sin's death penalty for us—in our place—then we would be saved from our predicament. But is there such a person? Thankfully, yes!

Meet your substitute—*Jesus Christ*. He is the One who took death's place for you!

> [God] made [Jesus Christ] who knew no sin to be sin on our behalf, so that we might become the righteousness of God in Him. (2 Corinthians 5:21)

God's Provision: A Savior

God rescued us by sending His Son, Jesus, to die on the cross for our sins (1 John 4:9–10). Jesus was fully human and fully divine (John 1:1, 18), a truth that ensures His understanding of our weaknesses, His power to forgive, and His ability to bridge the gap between God and us (Romans 5:6–11). In short, we are "justified as a gift by His grace through the redemption which is in Christ Jesus" (Romans 3:24). Two words in this verse bear further explanation: *justified* and *redemption*.

Justification is God's act of mercy, in which He declares believing sinners righteous while they are still in their sinning state. Justification doesn't mean that God *makes* us righteous, so that we never sin again, rather that He *declares* us righteous—much like a judge pardons a guilty criminal. Because Jesus took our sin upon Himself and suffered our judgment on the cross, God forgives our debt and proclaims us PARDONED.

Redemption is God's act of paying the ransom price to release us from our bondage to sin. Held hostage by Satan, we were shackled by the iron chains of sin and death. Like a loving parent whose child has been kidnapped, God willingly paid the ransom for you. And what a price He paid! He gave His only Son to bear our sins—past, present, and future. Jesus's death and resurrection broke our chains and set us free to become children of God (Romans 6:16–18, 22; Galatians 4:4–7).

PLACING YOUR FAITH IN CHRIST

These four truths describe how God has provided a way to Himself through Jesus Christ. Because the price has been paid in full by God, we must respond to His free gift of eternal life in total faith and confidence in Him to save us. We must step forward into the relationship with God that He has prepared for us—not by doing good works or by being good people, but by coming to Him just as we are and accepting His justification and redemption by faith.

> For by grace you have been saved through faith; and that not of yourselves, it is the gift of God; not as a result of works, so that no one may boast.
> (Ephesians 2:8–9)

We accept God's gift of salvation simply by placing our faith in Christ alone for the forgiveness of our sins. Would you like to enter into a relationship with your Creator by trusting in Christ as your Savior? If so, here's a simple prayer you can use to express your faith:

> *Dear God,*
>
> *I know that my sin has put a barrier between You and me. Thank You for sending Your Son, Jesus, to die in my place. I trust in Jesus alone to forgive my sins, and I accept His*

gift of eternal life. I ask Jesus to be my personal Savior and the Lord of my life. Thank You.

In Jesus's name, amen.

If you've prayed this prayer or one like it and you wish to find out more about knowing God and His plan for you in the Bible, contact us at Insight for Living. You can speak to one of our pastors on staff by calling 972-473-5097. Or you can write to us at the address below.

Pastoral Ministries Department
Insight for Living
Post Office Box 269000
Plano, Texas 75026-9000

ENDNOTES

Unless otherwise noted below, all material in this Bible Companion is adapted from the *Joseph: A Man of Integrity and Forgiveness* sermon series and companion book by Charles R. Swindoll and was supplemented by the Creative Ministries department of Insight for Living.

LESSON ONE

1. Joyce G. Baldwin, *The Message of Genesis 12–50*, The Bible Speaks Today (Downers Grove, Ill.: InterVarsity, 1986), 159.

LESSON TWO

Portions of this chapter have been adapted from *Cultivating Purity in an Impure World*, a LifeMaps book from the Bible-teaching ministry of Charles R. Swindoll (Plano, Tex.: IFL Publishing House, 2005).

1. Oscar Wilde, *The Picture of Dorian Gray* (New York: Barnes & Noble Books, 2003), 21.

2. Dietrich Bonhoeffer, *Creation and Fall: A Theological Interpretation of Genesis 1–3; Temptation* (New York: Macmillan/Collier Books, 1959), 116–117.

3. Clarence Edward Macartney, *Trials of Great Men of the Bible* (Nashville: Abingdon, 1946), 46.

4. Alfred Edersheim, *Bible History: Old Testament* (Grand Rapids: Eerdmans, 1987), 149.

5. Dag Hammarskjöld, *Markings*, trans. Leif Sjöberg and W. H. Auden (New York: Knopf, 1965), 15.

LESSON THREE

1. Viktor E. Frankl, *Man's Search for Meaning: An Introduction to Logotherapy*, 4th ed., part 1 trans. Ilse Lasch (Boston: Beacon, 1992), 75.

2. Betsie ten Boom, as quoted in Corrie ten Boom with John and Elizabeth Sherrill, *The Hiding Place*, 25th anniversary ed. (Grand Rapids: Chosen Books, 2003), 197.

LESSON FOUR

1. A. W. Tozer, *The Root of the Righteous* (Camp Hill, Pa.: Christian Publications, 1986), 137.

LESSON FIVE

1. J. Oswald Sanders, *Robust in Faith: Men from God's School* (Chicago: Moody Press, n.d.), 44.

2. Francis Brown, S. R. Driver, and Charles A. Briggs, eds., *The New Brown-Driver-Briggs-Gesenius Hebrew and English Lexicon* (Peabody, Mass.: Hendrickson, 1979), 371.

3. Brown, Driver, and Briggs, *The New Brown-Driver-Briggs-Gesenius Hebrew and English Lexicon*, 62, 415. See also Nahum M. Sarna, ed., *The JPS Torah Commentary: Genesis* (Philadelphia: The Jewish Publication Society, 1989), 210.

4. Sarna, *The JPS Torah Commentary: Genesis*, 287–288.

5. Flavius Josephus, *The Antiquities of the Jews*, in *Josephus: Complete Works*, 2.6.1, trans. William Whiston (Grand Rapids: Kregel, 1976), 49.

6. Brown, Driver, and Briggs, *The New Brown-Driver-Briggs-Gesenius Hebrew and English Lexicon*, 861.

7. Brown, Driver, and Briggs, *The New Brown-Driver-Briggs-Gesenius Hebrew and English Lexicon*, 62.

8. Brown, Driver, and Briggs, *The New Brown-Driver-Briggs-Gesenius Hebrew and English Lexicon*, 674.

9. Brown, Driver, and Briggs, *The New Brown-Driver-Briggs-Gesenius Hebrew and English Lexicon*, 826.

LESSON SIX

1. Frank Henry Cumbers and Frederick Brotherton Meyer, *Great Men of the Bible*, vol. 1 (Grand Rapids: Zondervan, 1981), 128–129. Used by permission.

LESSON SEVEN

1. Victor P. Hamilton, *The Book of Genesis: Chapters 18–50*, The New International Commentary on the Old Testament (Grand Rapids: Eerdmans, 1995), 541.

LESSON EIGHT

1. Philip Yancey, *What's So Amazing About Grace?* (Grand Rapids: Zondervan, 1997), 12. Used by permission.

2. William Shakespeare, *King Henry the Sixth, Part III*, 5.6.11, in *The Complete Works*, ed. Arthur Henry Bullen (New York: Barnes & Noble Books, 1994), 96.

3. Herodotus, *The Histories*, 2.41, trans. George Rawlinson (New York: Knopf, 1997), 143.

4. Nahum M. Sarna, ed., *The JPS Torah Commentary: Genesis* (Philadelphia: The Jewish Publication Society, 1989), 302.

5. Yancey, *What's So Amazing About Grace?* 12.

Lesson Nine

1.   Elbert Hubbard, *Selected Writings of Elbert Hubbard*, memorial ed. (New York: Wm. H. Wise, 1922), 58.

Lesson Ten

1.   Francis Brown, S.R. Driver, and Charles A. Briggs, eds., *The New Brown-Driver-Briggs-Gesenius Hebrew and English Lexicon* (Peabody, Mass.: Hendrickson, 1979), 919.

2.   Brown, Driver, and Briggs, *The New Brown-Driver-Briggs-Gesenius Hebrew and English Lexicon*, 806.

Lesson Eleven

1.   Phillips Brooks, "The Duty of the Business Man," in *Addresses* (Boston: Charles E. Brown & Co., 1893), 94.

2.   Brooks, "The Duty of the Business Man," 93.

3.   John C. Maxwell, *Developing the Leader within You* (Nashville: Thomas Nelson, 1993), 36.

4.   James Boswell, *The Life of Samuel Johnson* (London: Collins' Clear-Type Press, n.d.), 338.

Lesson Twelve

1.   Francis Brown, S.R. Driver, and Charles A. Briggs, eds., *The New Brown-Driver-Briggs-Gesenius Hebrew and English Lexicon* (Peabody, Mass.: Hendrickson, 1979), 138.

RESOURCES FOR PROBING FURTHER

In a society marked by scandal—political, corporate, and personal—where can we turn to find examples of integrity? In a culture characterized by lawsuits, revenge, and one-upmanship, who can we look to as a model of grace and forgiveness? In a nation lulled into a victim mentality, we need illustrations of men and women who live responsibly. Joseph is a remarkable example.

For further help in living a life of integrity and forgiveness, here are a few resources we would like to recommend. Of course, we cannot always endorse everything a writer or ministry says, so we encourage you to approach these and all other non-biblical resources with wisdom and discernment.

Bridges, Jerry. *Trusting God: Even When Life Hurts*. Colorado Springs: NavPress, 1990.

Dobson, James. *When God Doesn't Make Sense*. Wheaton, Ill.: Tyndale House, 1993.

Guinness, Os. *When No One Sees: The Importance of Character in an Age of Image*. Colorado Springs: NavPress, 2000.

Insight for Living. *Cultivating Purity in an Impure World* LifeMaps. Plano, Tex.: IFL Publishing House, 2005.

Patterson, Ben. *Waiting: Finding Hope When God Seems Silent*. Downers Grove, Ill.: InterVarsity, 1989.

Smalley, Gary and John Trent. *The Blessing*. Nashville: Thomas Nelson, 1986.

Swindoll, Charles R. *Joseph: A Man of Integrity and Forgiveness*. Nashville: Word Publishing, 1998.

Swindoll, Charles R. *The Grace Awakening: Believing in Grace Is One Thing. Living It Is Another*. Nashville: W Publishing, 2003.

Swindoll, Charles R. *The Quest for Character: Inspirational Thoughts for Becoming More Like Christ.* Grand Rapids: Zondervan, 1993.

Yancey, Philip. *Disappointment with God: Three Questions No One Asks Aloud.* Grand Rapids: Zondervan, 1988.

Yancey, Philip. *What's So Amazing about Grace?* Grand Rapids: Zondervan, 1997.

Yancey, Philip. *Where Is God When It Hurts?* anniversary ed. Grand Rapids: Zondervan, 2002.

Ordering Information

Joseph: A Man of Integrity and Forgiveness

If you would like to order additional Bible Companions, purchase the audio series that accompanies this Bible Companion, or request other products, please contact the office that serves you.

United States

Insight for Living
Post Office Box 269000
Plano, Texas 75026-9000
1-800-772-8888,
Monday through Thursday
7:00 a.m. – 9:00 p.m. and
Friday 7:00 a.m. – 7:00 p.m.
Central time
www.insight.org

Australia, New Zealand, and South Pacific

Insight for Living Australia
Post Office Box 1011
Bayswater, VIC 3153
AUSTRALIA
1300 467 444
www.insight.asn.au

Canada

Insight for Living Canada
Post Office Box 2510
Vancouver, BC V6B 3W7
1-800-663-7639
www.insightforliving.ca

United Kingdom and Europe

Insight for Living United Kingdom
Post Office Box 348
Leatherhead
KT22 2DS
UNITED KINGDOM
0800 915 9364
www.insightforliving.org.uk

Other International Locations

International constituents may contact the U.S. office through our Web site (www.insight.org), mail queries, or by calling +1-972-473-5136.